A COLLECTOR'S GUIDE TO TEA SILVER
1670–1900

A Collector's
Guide to
TEA SILVER
1670–1900

ELIZABETH DE CASTRES

FREDERICK MULLER LIMITED
LONDON

First published in Great Britain 1977
by Frederick Muller Limited, London, NW2 6LE

ISBN 0 584 10289 5

British Library Cataloguing in Publication Data

De Castres, Elizabeth
    A collector's guide to tea silver, 1670–1900.
    1. Silverware, English – History   2. Tea making
    paraphernalia – England – History
    I. Title
    739.2'3'742   NK7144

    ISBN 0–584–10289–5

Printed in Great Britain by The Anchor Press Ltd
and bound by Wm Brendon & Son Ltd
both of Tiptree, Essex

CONTENTS

LIST OF ILLUSTRATIONS

ACKNOWLEDGEMENTS

The author would like to express her gratitude to Janet Dunbar, S. A. G. Twining Esq., and J. G. Shearlock Esq., for their help and guidance, and also the following for their kind assistance with illustrations: Christie's, J. H. Bourdon-Smith Ltd., Garrard and Company Ltd., Captain J. G. Norie, Phillips, S. J. Shrubsole Ltd., Sotheby and Company, Spink and Son Ltd., The Victoria and Albert Museum and the Worshipful Company of Goldsmiths.

To G.W.W. who helped minimise the problems.

Now stir the fire, and close the shutters
    fast,
Let fall the curtains, wheel the sofa
    round,
And, while the bubbling and loud
    hissing urn
Throws up a steamy column, and the
    cups,
That cheer but not inebriate, wait on
    each,
So let us welcome peaceful evening in.

William Cowper

INTRODUCTION

Tea is a universal beverage. It is brewed in tea pots, tea urns and tea cups; drunk with milk, lemon, mint, jasmine or even rancid yak butter. Some 2,624 million pounds of it are produced throughout the world each year, and although ways of making it can vary considerably from country to country, the satisfaction derived from a well-made cup of tea is a pleasure enjoyed by all.

In England and America we are comparative newcomers to the beverage, which is believed to have originated in China probably around 2,750 years before the birth of Christ. By the 8th century A.D., however, tea was enjoyed by most Chinese and also had a reputation for its medicinal values. In Japan, too, it was introduced at an early date.

Gradually tea drinking spread to the West, but it was not until the 17th century that it began to establish itself in England. Tea was on sale in London certainly before the Restoration, although in its early days only the wealthy could afford it.

The earliest known English silver tea pot can be seen at the Victoria and Albert Museum (see plate No. 1). It was made in 1670 and does not seem much like a tea pot by our standards. Instead it resembles more a coffee pot, with a tall, cylinder-shaped body, tapering sides and a conical cover, topped by a small baluster finial. The handle, which is at right angles to the spout, is partly covered in leather.

One of the earliest known American tea pots was made by Jacob Boelen of New York during the first few years of the 18th century (The Metropolitan Museum of Art, New York) and is a beautiful little vessel, some 16·5 cm (6½ inches) high with an elaborate cartouche. The cover is gadrooned and has naturalistic ornament, while the base has a simple geometric pattern. Earlier mention of an American tea pot is recorded in the inventory of the lieutenant governor of Massachusetts, Sir William Stoughton, who possessed one certainly before 1701.

In 1773 a tax on tea was one of the factors which led to the American War of Independence. At that time all goods exported from Britain to America were taxed, but the policy was revised and duties were dropped, except those on tea. The British Government had decided to continue to tax tea to establish their right to exact taxes on the colonies. Although the amount was meagre, it was the principle behind the decision which provoked such strong feeling.

At Boston in 1773, a crowd converged on the harbour and stormed aboard ships carrying tea. The cargoes were thrown into the sea by quite an orderly mob who appeared to have planned their manoeuvres most thoroughly. Altogether 342 chests of tea worth £10,000 were ejected. More demonstrations followed and people refused to drink tea. The British Government decided to close the port of Boston and troops were sent to the city. This incited open revolt which led to the War of Independence.

Today, roughly 140 million pounds' worth of tea is sold through grocery outlets in America, and the growth rate, at the time of going to press, is nearly 8 per cent, exceeding all other beverages in that country with the sole exception of orange juice.

Apart from being drunk as a refreshing "pick-me-up" by millions throughout the world during their ordinary daily lives, tea occupies a more important social position based on hundreds of years of tradition. Despite the pressures of modern living, having friends to tea is a form of entertaining which most of us still enjoy, just as our ancestors did before us. A pride in the silver used at tea time is as strong as ever, and although this book is intended primarily for collectors, those seeking to buy tea silver for themselves or as a present, or who are merely interested in its origins, can greatly benefit by studying the fascinating development of style and decoration.

Most women have a good china tea service, and what better to complement this than a glittering silver tea pot, jug and sugar bowl? Among other things, this book seeks to dispel the myth that you have to be rich to buy old silver. Antique sugar tongs and spoons can still be bought for reasonable prices, and while certain objects do undoubtedly cost far more than most people could afford, even these can be bought for more modest amounts in old Sheffield plate or good 19th century electro-plate. The latter, which can still be found for a song, may well become a collectable of tomorrow.

These pages are concerned with practically all types of silver which have been connected with the tea-time ritual over the years. A great attraction of such silver is that it is still eminently functional. A caddy spoon today, while being just as beautiful as when it was first made, unlike many objects of comparable vintage, is still useful. While it would be foolhardy to exploit this with some of the rare collectors' items, to use such objects occasionally with care can do little harm.

Modern tea pots have altered little from many 18th century examples; milk jugs are still similar in plan to their earlier counterparts; and sugar bowls today fulfil their identical purpose. Thus, tea silver, once invested in, should be a thing of beauty and usefulness not only to its present owner but to future generations. It has a timeless quality. This is one of the factors which make it so collectable; a good investment; excellent as a present and a thoroughly worthwhile addition to any home. Its beauty once observed remains with one, imparting an elegance and graciousness well deserved by such an ancient custom.

The general social and economic growth of both England and America through the centuries has resulted in an ever-increasing demand for domestic silver, and although the first English tea pot was made towards the end of the 17th century, most English tea silver which is collected today dates from about 1770. By that time new methods of manufacture were making possible the production of cheaper, less expensive pieces of tea equipage which accelerated its demand.

Early methods of manufacture were primitive. The silver was reduced from the ingot to the required thickness by the laborious application of a heavy hammer. Pieces cut from this flattened sheet were then raised from the flat, as it is called, by hand-hammering on the sinking block. This was a block shaped into various circular forms. Gradually the required hollow form would be achieved. As repeated hammering makes silver brittle, the metal needed to be continuously annealed. Finally a planishing hammer would smooth out any irregularities, rendering the surface even and radiant. Adjoining parts like a hollow foot would be similarly produced and soldered on. Handles, finials and so on were shaped by casting. Simple forms of ornament might decorate cast pieces, perhaps scrolls in low relief on a spoon bowl.

London silversmiths set the standards of workmanship, style and decoration. Silversmiths in America followed them. The latter worked in the leading and growing cities of Boston, Philadelphia and New York, and in their turn set the standards for craftsmen in the urban centres of America. These wealthy cities maintained a very close link with London, the majority of their inhabitants having, of course, emigrated from England. Thus all contacts with the mother country, whether of an artistic or social nature, were inevitably firm and deep.

In the New World, as with the old country, silver was looked upon as something more than a functional necessity. Acquisition of it automatically accounted for immediate social prestige. The more a person owned, the better his social standing. This did not only apply to the *nouveau riche*. Noblemen from ancient families, whose social standing none could doubt, still contributed in no small measure to this school of thought, filling their vast mansions with a veritable surfeit of domestic silver, not to mention silver furniture. Silver, after all, could always be melted down, and sold to pay more pressing debts. Nevertheless, despite the early increase in the demand for domestic silver generally, only a very small minority, either in England or America, were in the happy financial position to be able to avail themselves of its splendour. Many decades were to pass before its advantages could be shared by the less wealthy.

Meanwhile cyclic fashions dictated various forms and shapes, embellished with certain types of decoration. As early, heavy-gauge silver did not lend itself so well to embossing, engraving was an alternative method of decorating. The engraver worked with various pointed tools to cut away the surface into the required pattern. Engraving is not always easy to distinguish from flat chasing, however, which is a method used to achieve comparable decorative effects by hammer and punches. While the piece was being chased, a filling of pitch amalgam would be used to keep the shape of the hollow vessel. The engraver, working with his pointed tools, required less pressure as he cut away the metal instead of hammering it, so he would rest the piece on some form of pad. Chasing would be applied only to the front of pieces. Embossing or *repoussé* work necessitated pressure being applied from the back.

Cut-card work, although usually attributed to the Huguenot immigrant silversmiths, first appeared long before their arrival. It can be seen on a pair of small covered cups, circa 1667, in the Ashmolean Museum, Oxford. It consisted of applying, by soldering, cut-out work taken from a separate sheet of silver. The effect of this applied form of decoration was that although it was actually flat, it showed in relief against the surface of the object. Considerable skill was necessary in the use of solder at the right temperature, particularly with later, more elaborate work. In fact, so skilful became the craftsmen using this method, that it is sometimes quite difficult to distinguish it from cast decoration.

Very early cut-card work was quite plain and generally narrow, usually in foliate patterns. It was often used to encircle the base of vessels just above the foot-ring. During the Britannia standard period (see chapter on hall-marks), cut-card work might envelope the lower half of the body of a piece. It was also used on the covers and to strengthen the junction where handles joined the bodies. A further development was in the application of separate leaves, soldered one upon the other, the whole effect being one of superlative delicacy. Another variation consisted of the plain cut-card work being surface-ornamented with applied cast motifs, perhaps small beading. Sometimes these might also be chased or engraved in the applied metal, instead of being only cast. Thus leaf-shapes were often decorated with engraved veins or mid-ribs.

Early piercing, later to be developed by mechanical means, was cut by a fret-saw. Because so much of the silver was inevitably cut away, some form of strengthening was essential, and this was achieved usually by deeply convex embossing.

Silversmithing methods changed little during the first few decades of the 18th century. Decoration continued generally along the lines already mentioned. The rococo style which came into being quite early in the century lasted with vigour until the dawn of the neo-classical period, around 1760. Main rococo characteristics are asymmetrical forms and ornament with C and S scrolls, rock motifs, shell outlines and the popular *chinoiseries*. Rococo-inspired decoration appeared not only on tea silver, it pervaded the full gamut of products to emerge from the silversmith's workshop. Even the covers of casters echoed in their ornate pierced work the fashion for rococo asymmetry. Elaborately pierced cake baskets followed suit, together with tea pots, tea kettles, milk jugs, caddies and sugar bowls, which all came under the influence of this ebullient style of decoration.

One of the most important developments in the production of silver was the metal rolling-mill, which was invented in the final years of the 17th century and greatly improved upon during the following one. These improvements meant that an unheated ingot of silver could be passed repeatedly through rollers, finally to emerge a smooth piece of metal of uniform gauge. A far cry from the sledge-hammer employed for so many years by silversmiths generally. One immediate result was the production of far less expensive silver; less expensive because not only had the number of man-hours previously required been considerably reduced, but also the actual silver was automatically less costly, being so much lighter in weight.

By the 1760's the neo-classical movement was already making itself felt in the silversmith's workshop. Yet, despite the fact that the name of Robert Adam has become synonymous with this period, neither he nor his brother James appear to have been commissioned by any silversmith. They did, however, produce drawings for silver, when asked to do so by wealthy clients. Fine Adam-style tea silver of an early vintage was originally made by London silversmiths, but this was to quickly alter as the Birmingham and Sheffield silversmiths came into their own with new, speedy methods made possible by developments in machines.

During the last three decades of the 18th century, Birmingham and Sheffield grew to unprecedented importance, so much so that both were permitted to open assay offices in 1773. Silver chattels had always been an important status symbol, and quite apart from the new machines which enabled the production of less expensive domestic silver, the advent of Sheffield plate had also added enormously to the output from these two towns.

Outside Sheffield, Matthew Boulton's Soho works in Birmingham became the major factory for the new plate. Having gone himself initially to Sheffield to learn the intricacies of producing Sheffield plate, Boulton returned to his home town and set up a factory from which were to come some of the finest examples of this type of work. An amazing variety of objects was made there, incorporating all types of domestic items. Among these were some very fine sugar baskets of wire, lined with blue glass. They were often elaborately decorated with fine stamped-out leaves, flowers and wire tendrils, expertly soldered together. Cake baskets, too, were exquisitely made. Examples show that some of these were actually produced by the age-old method of hammering up from the flat and then cutting the plated metal with a fret-saw. Others were produced from machine-rolled silver and automatically pierced.

New methods included stamping, with drop hammers and fly punches, pieces which had previously required shaping by hand. The new, thin silver made possible by developments in the rolling process meant that entire sections of a vessel like a straight-sided tea pot could be stamped out with dies and soldered together. Decorative effects might be achieved by stamping this fine-gauge silver in low relief between appropriately sunk dies, or perhaps by cutting a series of open-work patterns, achieved by simply varying the punches. Mechanical piercing meant that more people could avail themselves of a sugar basket or similar object. The whole effect looked extremely attractive set against a blue glass liner, even if the actual work lacked the quality of the hand-made article.

Towards the last few years of the 18th century, the development of a harder steel resulted in further progress in mass-production. The steel tool contained in the fly-press could now be worked for far longer runs without its outline becoming blurred, also making possible more elaborate patterns. By the last quarter of the 18th century, Matthew Boulton and his partner John Fothergill had installed at their Soho works enough of the new equipment to enable them to mass-produce unfinished parts and to sell them to other firms for assembly and finishing.

A most popular form of decoration to become fashionable during the final years of the 18th century was the engraving technique known as bright-cutting. The charming, faceted effect of bright-cutting was achieved by special gouges. Much of this work is extremely fine and delicate. Tea services and various other pieces of tea equipage bear much evidence of it, including tea spoons, caddy spoons and sugar tongs.

Neo-classical shapes of tea silver were elegant with contrasting sweeping lines and graduated curves, combining vertical and horizontal straight lines. Many tea pots of the period were oval, octangular, circular or shaped with vertical sides, all lending themselves perfectly to the new stamping-out processes. Jugs became similarly graceful in outline, as did tea urns and caddies. The latter were quite commonly based on the Adam vase, their proportions somewhat inaccurate. These might be embossed and ring handles added. The box-type of tea caddy was often exquisitely decorated with bright-cutting. Towards the later years of this period, the silver tea service made its appearance. Before this, the service as such had been comparatively unknown. The production of cheaper, thinner-gauge silver now made the production of a matching set economically viable. Once introduced, tea services remained popular for the next hundred years or so. They were not always to be produced in sterling silver. Instead Sheffield plate might be used, and later the 19th century discovery of the process known as electro-deposition enabled the production of an amazing variety of shapes and styles, at prices which the masses could afford.

Thus, the Regency period arrived on a tide of miscellaneous tea silver, flowing from the factory at an unprecedented rate and with its popularity ascending at a likewise pace. Such phenomenal success augured well for the future of domestic silver. By the first few years of the 19th century progress was being made in electro-metallurgy, and further experiments were to show later that it was also possible to produce an even cheaper version of Sheffield plate.

Meanwhile the Regency era with all its opulence was gathering rapid momentum, yet despite this there were no signs of any particular style in domestic silver emerging. Tea pots followed this vague tendency as much as any other object; milk jugs mirrored the diverse shapes of tea pots and were generally rather low; sugar basins became a little larger, their outlines matching those of the milk jugs, their two opposed handles usually of the same design as those on the jugs; hot water jugs, although not unlike the tea pot, were generally proportionately taller, and some which were very similar to the tea pot as far as the shoulder, altered above this point, their necks becoming elongated. Those with pedestals were based on classical tripod forms with paw feet. Some had tripod stands with a spirit burner below, and in these examples the burners might be shaped like the bodies of classical lamps.

By the third decade of the 19th century, the Romantic movement began to influence decoration, bringing with it ornaments of a modified classical or 18th century nature. These were combined with current ideas and paved the way for the Victorian era with its audacious, uninhibited simulation of all that had gone before in style, form and decoration. The result, which is dealt with fully in the chapter on Victorian silver, was a fantastic medley of design, possessing neither the discipline nor the style of any particular period. Despite this the Victorian years proved to be a natural step in the evolution of the story as a whole, and as such deserve recognition for the part they played.

CHAPTER ONE

TEA POTS

"Now for the tea of our host,
Now for the rollicking bun,
Now for the muffin and toast,
Now for the gay Sally Lunn!"

W. S. Gilbert

Few would have dreamed that tea with such unpretentious and modest beginnings would grow to play so important a role in the social life of ensuing generations. This unassuming beverage slipped quietly on to the scene in England at least as early as 1658, making very little impact and causing at first only a modicum of interest among a small section of the community, namely the very wealthy, who were the only people able to afford it.

A tea advertisement which appeared in the *London Gazette* in 1658, and which is probably the earliest reference to tea in this context, declares "That Excellent, and by all Physitians approved, China Drink, called by the Chineans, Tcha, by other Nations Tay, alias Tee, is sold at the Sultaness-head, a Cophee-house, in Sweetings Rents by the Royal Exchange, London." In this same issue is reported the death of Oliver Cromwell.

In September 1660, Samuel Pepys wrote in his diary, "I did send for a cup of tee (a China drink) of which I never had drunk before."

Nine years later the East India Company first imported tea. This small amount of two canisters from Bantam containing $143\frac{1}{2}$ pounds was really used only for the refreshment of the committee at East India House, or perhaps given away as presents. A further nine years were to pass before, in 1678, tea finally became an import in its own right. The total imported for the year was

4,713 pounds. By 1700 this had grown to 20,000 pounds, and within twenty-one years it had exceeded 1,000,000 pounds.

Thomas Twining, the founder of the famous tea and coffee merchants, first started on his venture to sell tea by opening his own coffee-house at Devereux Court, Strand, in 1706. By 1717 the tea trade at Tom's had made such excellent progress that a separate house adjoining his original coffee-house was necessary to deal with the expanding business. The word "tip" is said to have originated in those early coffee-houses, of which there were thought to be over 2,000 in the early years of the 18th century. Nailed to the walls were boxes in which customers requiring speedy service placed a little extra money for the facility. On each box were the words, "to insure promptness", the initial spelling of t.i.p.

Until this time, and with the exception of the cider drinking counties, ale had occupied an unchallenged position as the main drink of man, woman and child. Not unnaturally, drunkenness was the common vice of the day. The arrival of tea and coffee were to lessen this considerably, although the introduction of cheap spirits contributed towards its increase at a later stage.

Meanwhile, tea was gradually becoming a fashion in high society. Favoured by Charles II's queen, Catherine of Braganza, it appeared increasingly in the great houses of the aristocracy. Brewed in the Chinese manner and drunk from porcelain pots, its delicate flavour was relished by all those able to avail themselves of it. Rare examples of these early porcelain pots in silver mounts date from towards the last few decades of the 17th century.

In 1660, at Garraway's in Exchange Alley, tea was being sold in leaf at from 15s to 50s per pound. Garraway's, which was patronised by rich merchants, sold drugs, timber and wine by candle-light in the big sale rooms. An Act of Parliament of 1660 levied a duty of eighteenpence on every gallon of tea made for sale.

By 1670 the first tea pot finally made its appearance (see plate No. 1); a strange-looking specimen, easily mistaken for a coffee pot, it is now in the Victoria and Albert Museum. If it were not for the inscription on it which makes it perfectly clear that it was intended for tea, it might never have come to be associated with the beverage. In fact, very few silver tea pots seem to have been made in England before the reign of Queen Anne, and possibly the earliest example to look anything like the tea pot with which we have become familiar is a decidedly melon-shaped vessel made by Charles Shelley, which appears to have been produced some time before 1679. It has a narrow, recurving spout and a wooden handle pinned into two silver sockets. There are also two gilt examples of about 1685, both melon-shaped, the rotundity of which seems to have developed from the Chinese wine pot. Both of these tea pots are under 15 cms (6 inches) high, shaped into segments from top to base to resemble the fruit, the spouts curving gracefully from a low point on the body, opposite the handle, and the high line of the domed lid incorporated in the general melon shape. There is an example of these both at the Victoria and Albert Museum and the Ashmolean Museum, Oxford.

By the time Queen Anne came to the throne the future of tea was virtually assured, although tea pots were still very much in their early stages. Some examples of this period continued to be melon-shaped, although squatter in outline than the original versions. Becoming far more common, however, was the new pear-shape or pyriform body. These might be either round or octagonal, their graceful curving spouts sometimes culminating in a bird's head. Early examples might have their handles set at right angles to the spout, which must have proved rather inconvenient. Happily, the handle soon found its correct place opposite the spout, no doubt to the relief of many a hostess. Sometimes these delightful pear-shaped tea pots came equipped with a spirit lamp and stand; more often than not these are missing today. These early examples were extremely charming with good proportions, devoid as they usually were of much decoration and relying purely on their shape for effect. There are some specimens which have been decorated by Huguenot silversmiths with cut-card work.

The immigrant Huguenot silversmiths who fled to England after the Revocation of the Edict of Nantes (1685) had among their numbers many expert and skilled craftsmen. Despite hostility from London silversmiths they eventually received recognition. The high quality of their work greatly influenced English craftsmen.

Huguenot silversmiths of importance during this early period included David Willaume and Pierre Platel. Apprenticed to the former was Louise Mettayer, while the man who later became the most famous of them all, Paul de Lamerie, was apprenticed to Pierre Platel. Although Lamerie is now associated with elaborate work, he also made many simple pieces, particularly during his early, formative years. Later he was commissioned by the wealthiest in the land, and began to produce the masterpieces with which he has become associated. Many such pieces were not to appear for several years.

Garrard's, the famous London silversmiths and jewellers, is one of the few firms now in existence which can trace their history back to this early period, to George Wickes, who entered his mark in 1721.

The little pear-shaped tea pots so apparent on the tea scene of those days, often standing no more than a diminutive 15 cms (6 inches) high, remained in fashion for about the first quarter of the 18th century. General characteristics included a hinged, domed lid with a finial of metal or with a wooden knop to prevent the fingers from being burned; simple wooden handles, sometimes curved, plain or covered in leather, pinned into circular sockets; and shaped or faceted spouts emerging roughly from the centre of the pear-shaped bulge, the outlet still shaped as a bird's head, sometimes described as that of a duck, goose or even swan. The spout might sometimes be equipped with a small hinged flap at its opening, presumably to help keep its contents hot. Spout caps on very early pots were attached by chains.

During the second decade of the 18th century a new form appeared. This was the global or bullet-shaped tea pot, which may be described as the forerunner of the tea pot as we really know it today. It was not completely spherical in shape, however, although the Scottish silversmiths came very close to it with their examples. The global shape actually made its debut as early as 1716, and there is in existence a fine specimen by the Huguenot silversmith Paul de Lamerie of this time. An even earlier example by the English silversmith Anthony Nelme was made in 1712. Generally speaking, however, the globular pot did not become fashionable until several years later, eventually replacing altogether the pear-shaped variety. It stood on a narrow, moulded ring base. Its top was flattish, and into this line the lid sometimes fitted flush or was slightly moulded. A finial topped this cover. Usually the handles were of wood, and unlike that of the pear-shaped pot, the spout was generally straight, tapering acutely from a moulded joint. The Scottish spherical version possessed a similar spout. Unlike its English counterpart, this pot stood upon a stemmed foot, a style which never seems to have been taken up by Georgian silversmiths in England. Any decoration would usually be flat chasing, at which the silversmiths of the period were most adept, producing as they did some superlative work.

In those early days the making of tea was an important social ritual. It was always freshly infused in a gracious manner by the hostess herself, a servant appearing silently with the boiling water for the mistress to perform the exacting task of brewing the delectable concoction.

Some tea pots had a handled tripod stand, mounted over a spirit lamp, as can be seen in the reproduction of the oil painting by Richard Collins (see plate No. 2); painted in about 1725, it is generally thought to be of the Gay family. They drink from oriental-style handleless bowls, holding them with care, presumably because they were probably both expensive and hot to the touch; there is a covered sugar bowl, charming hexagonal tea canister with a domed lid, hot milk or water jug, voiding bowl, and a pear-shaped tea pot and spirit lamp on a stand. The cover of the voiding bowl appears to be in use as a tray for spoons.

The demand for American silver came, as with England, from the sophisticated and wealthy sections of the community, who were to be found in or around the three main cities of Boston, New York and Philadelphia. It was in these prosperous and growing towns that most of the good silver was produced. Although Newport and Baltimore both had productive silversmiths, their work is not generally regarded as of such importance.

Because most of the original settlers, except in New York, had emigrated from England, the English influence in all things artistic and cultural was naturally very strong. This influence played a prominent role in the styles and design of silver; the first American craftsmen following quite rigidly the shapes and decorations being produced in London. Also, the silver which early English settlers had brought with them like spoons, bowls, casters and jugs, were naturally the first to be copied.

Thus when tea drinking came to England, and specialised tea silver gradually evolved for its infusion, the same ideas were

27

imported into America, and tea pots across the Atlantic greatly resembled those by London makers. But this applies not only to tea silver. During those early years practically all American silver derived its inspiration from London. Wealthy Americans able to afford the luxury of silver wanted the same as their affluent counterparts in England.

In the Yale University Art Gallery, New Haven, Connecticut (the Mabel Brady Garven Collection), there are two pear-shaped tea pots made by Peter van Dyck which well illustrate this English influence. One is octagonal with a flowing scroll-shaped handle and octagonal-shaped spout, culminating in the shape of a bird's head; the other is similar except that it is round. The same collection has an excellent example of a globular tea pot by Jacob Hurd. The lid fits flush into the flattish top and the wooden handle is plain and unadorned. A coat of arms and cartouche are the only decorations, with the exception of a simple pattern on the lid and top of the body. Although very early Boston tea pots followed the pear-shape outline, hardly any examples remain today; most are of a later date, as with the one by Jacob Hurd, and follow the English globular, bullet or apple-shape.

By the 1730's the ebullience of French rococo was strengthening its influence. Elaborate designs based on flowers and scrolls were extravagantly used with great panache. At the same time other examples might be left in their unadorned state. Those that did come under its influence might have spouts shaped like dragons, and certainly the ubiquitous pineapple (symbol of hospitality) commonly adorned practically all covers. The rococo style is typified by C and S scrolls, and rock and shell motifs, the name rococo being derived from the French word for rock-work, *rocaille*. Shapes generally were subservient to the glories of the decoration. Tea pots of a particularly distinctive or ornate design would be made to a customer's special commission, both in England and America. This was the usual practice for an unusual or particularly expensive item of silver. Silversmiths usually stocked only the more mundane bread-and-butter lines, and not too many of these, either. Thus there is happily quite a lot of early silver which is completely individual, made for a specific order, although it might be based on some comparable piece.

Meanwhile the number of silversmiths was growing. By 1761,

the Goldsmiths' Company in the City of London had a membership of three hundred, a Prime Warden and three more Wardens. There were ninety-eight assistants and a livery of one hundred and ninety-eight members, who each paid £20 upon admission, a great deal of money then.

The earliest form of rococo decoration in America appears on a tea pot by Jacob Hurd. American silversmiths famous for their rococo work include Benjamin Burt and Paul Revere, both of Boston. An interesting fact about the former is that while he was a veritable giant of a man, reputed to have weighed around 180 kg (400 pounds), his work in contrast to his physique was extremely fine and delicate. A typical example is the beautiful tea pot made by him in 1765, to be seen at the Yale University Art Gallery, New Haven, Connecticut (Mabel Brady Garven Collection). The proportions are superb and the decoration extremely tasteful and delicate. The cover has a pineapple finial. American tea pots of the rococo period followed generally the inverted pyriform shape which had appeared in England towards the end of George II's reign, and which was set upon a drop-bottom, raised on a stem and moulded foot. Another fine example of the period by Peter de Riemer can be seen at the Museum of the City of New York. It was made as part of a matching tea set including sugar bowl and milk jug, and, in fact, is of a more distinctive rococo decoration than Burt's tea pot, which already seems to have come under the influence of the neo-classical. Rococo tea sets were made in greater quantity by this time and there are some fine examples from all three of the main centres; where the complete sets may not have survived there usually remains the tea pot or the sugar bowl or cream jug to give justice to the fine workmanship.

In England, leading exponents of the rococo style included Paul de Lamerie and Charles and Frederick Kandler, who both produced spectacular and highly imaginative work, beautifully executed. Others followed suit and the period proved to be one of astounding richness and diversity which, surprisingly, came quite suddenly to an end in roughly 1770, when it was totally eclipsed by the neo-classical era.

Running concurrently with the scroll and floral motifs of the rococo style during the middle of the century and later were the orientally inspired form of decoration known as *chinoiseries*. These were pure fantasy; imagined Chinese-type characters and other decorative effects complemented by a variety of scrolls, shells, asymmetrical cartouches and rock-like patterns. A Chinaman, shaped in full relief, often completed the effect.

Until about 1760, the body of the tea pot was hammered up from the flat, beaten out of the solid silver metal until the thickness was reduced and the shape gradually formed. This method was costly, and therefore when neo-classical designs created so much impact, silversmiths were only too pleased to avail themselves of the opportunity to produce the new straight-sided pots which then became fashionable, and which could be so easily produced from sheet silver, rolled to a very thin gauge by the rolling-mill. In doing this they immediately reduced the cost of the object, at the same time increasing their volume of work because more people could afford silver.

The new neo-classical tea pots appeared in circular, oval or polygonal shapes. Bases were flat and sides vertical. Lids might be a little domed; handles were arched or scrolled and spouts tapered. Often the bodies were delicately engraved, and general ornament included vertical or spiral palmettes and acanthus leaves, shallow fluting, *paterae*, rams' heads, the key pattern, running floral scrolls, laurel wreaths, swags of foliage or cloth and ribbon bows. Mouldings commonly were beading, astragals and reeding.

The neo-classical movement had strong ties with the work of one man in particular, the architect and designer, Robert Adam, whose influence was felt universally. He travelled extensively in Italy during the 1750's and on his return was appointed architect to George III. The Adam style has become synonymous with the term neo-classical, the first signs of which appeared in architecture, followed by interior decoration and then by domestic objects. The new shapes relied on perfection in balance, with graceful, sweeping curves and elegant outlines. They were in complete contrast to the rococo movement, during which the actual shape was of secondary importance to the decoration.

The demand for tea pots was growing. By the early 1760's tea drinking had set in as a national habit, even though the cost was still high. From 1750 to 1783, the price of teas sold by the East

India Company averaged around four and sixpence a pound, but duties raised the average wholesale price to over seven and six-pence a pound. Small wonder that the idea of the working class squandering their money on such luxuries struck a note of discord.

Arthur Young, in his *Farmer's Letters* for 1767, expresses irritation that "as much superfluous money is expended on tea and sugar as would maintain four million more subjects on bread".

His words went unheeded, however, and the astronomical ascent in the sale of tea continued, as Sir Frederick Eden revealed in 1797. "Any person who will give himself the trouble of stepping into the cottages of Middlesex and Surrey at meal times, will find that in poor families tea is not only the usual beverage in the morning and evening, but is generally drank in large quantities at dinner."

Even as early as 1743, Duncan Forbes, Lord President of the Court of Session, wrote to Lord Tweeddale: "Tea . . . is now become so common that the meanest familys, even of labouring people, particularly in Burroughs, make their morning's Meal of it, and thereby wholly disuse the ale, which heretofore was their accustomed drink; and the same Drug supplies all the labouring women with their afternoons' entertainments . . ."

Further ineffectual indignation came from Jonas Hanway some fourteen years later. "To what a height of folly must a nation be arrived, when the common people are not satisfied with whole-some food at home, but must go to the remotest regions to please a vicious palate! There is a certain lane near Richmond where beggars are often seen, in the summer season, drinking their tea. You may see labourers who are mending the roads drinking their tea; it is even drank in cinder-carts; and what is no less absurd, sold out of cups to hay-makers."

Even the boys at Eton had taken to the beverage. In Maxwell Lyte's *History of Eton*, a pupil writes to his father in 1766, declaring with feeling, "I wish you would be so kind as to let me have Tea and Sugar here to drink in the afternoon, without which there is no such thing as keeping company with other boys of my standing."

During the first half of the 18th century, tea pots and other items of tea equipage were usually of silver in the households of the wealthy and fashionable. It was to these silver designs that

31

early potters turned for inspiration, producing shapes of similar form in earthenware and later in porcelain.

An early Astbury-Whieldon tea pot in lead-glazed earthenware with relief decoration, circa 1740, follows exactly the shape of the globular tea pot then so fashionable. A charming Caughley pot with stand, circa 1775, is a replica of the flat-topped barrel shape which was copied a great deal by potters.

Although there were a number of women silversmiths during these years, by far the most famous of them was Hester Bateman. Silver was produced under her mark, which was first registered in 1761, for nearly 30 years. Hester Bateman was a unique woman. She built up a thriving business with a fine reputation for the highest quality of work, and later her sons, daughter-in-law and grandsons worked with her. She retired in 1790 and for a while work was produced bearing the mark of Peter and Jonathan. When Jonathan died shortly after, Peter and Ann registered their mark. From the Batemans came a variety of superb tea pots, beautifully executed, some exquisitely bright-cut often with beaded edges.

Many early neo-classical silver tea pots possessed neither foot-ring nor feet at the base of the pot. Hardly surprising, therefore, was the fact that when these were filled with hot tea they left unsightly marks on the polished surfaces of tables. It was to eliminate this, no doubt, that a silver stand on four moulded feet or spherical shapes was made to place beneath the pot. By the turn of the 19th century, the stand was discarded and four feet were placed on the base of the tea pot itself.

A magnificent example of a neo-classical tea pot and stand by Andrew Fogelberg and Stephen Gilbert, circa 1784, can be seen at the Victoria and Albert Museum. The ornate stand upon ball feet has elegant, tapering legs joined at the base by curved beading. Rams' heads surmount each of the legs which are linked by swags. This superb tea pot is decorated with classical motifs, and has only one flaw, a rounded base, which must have made it quite lethal to use, unless replaced immediately on its stand. Another tea pot by the same makers, also at the Victoria and Albert Museum, identical in appearance but made three years earlier, has a foot rim. One may conjecture that too many burned table-tops resulted from this style, which perhaps is why the makers

1. The earliest known silver tea pot, now in the Victoria and Albert Museum. It was presented to the Committee of the East India Company in 1670 by Lord Berkeley who was on the Committee from 1660 until 1697. (Victoria and Albert Museum)

2. This pyriform tea pot was made during the reign of George I in 1718 and bears an Exeter mark. (Garrard and Company Ltd.)

3. An oil painting by Richard Collins c. 1725, showing silver tea equipage of the George I period, including, left to right, a covered sugar bowl, hexagonal tea canister with domed lid, hot milk (or hot water) jug, voiding bowl and pyriform tea pot on a stand with a spirit lamp. Thought to be of the Gay family, the painting shows how tea was originally drunk from handleless porcelain cups. (Victoria and Albert Museum)

4. Late 18th century neo-classical tea pot by Hester Bateman. (S. J. Shrubsole Ltd.)

5. This Queen Anne tea canister was made in 1710 by Thomas Ash. It stands 5 in high and weighs 8 oz, and is marked on the side, base and sliding cover. It bears the crest of 'a Talbot's head erased and collared'. (J. H. Bourdon-Smith Ltd.)

6. A set of vase-shaped tea and sugar
canisters in ogee outline by Samuel
Taylor, 1748. (Phillips)

7. A magnificent neo-classical tea caddy by
Andrew Fogelberg and Stephen Gilbert,
1786. This splendid design was adapted
into a tea pot, now in the collection of the
Victoria and Albert museum. (Spink and
Son Ltd.)

8. A rare set of tea equipage bearing the arms of the Prince Regent, made in London in 1793 and including tea caddies, sugar bowl, sugar tongs, mote skimmer, spoon and muffineer. (S. J. Shrubsole Ltd.)

9. An early silver tea cup with flat chased chinoiseries, made during the reign of Charles II in 1683. (Garrard and Company Ltd.)

10. A rare, fluted cup and saucer with scalloped edges, made by Mark Paillet, London 1700. (University of Bath)

11. Birmingham caddy spoons, centre, George III small chased circular bowl, snake handle, by Matthew Linwood, 1807; left to right: George III hooded shell, ivory handle, John Lawrence and Co., 1809; William IV engraved scoop bowl, hollow king's pattern handle, Taylor and Perry, 1835; George IV 'bread pan' stained wood handle, J.H. (incised), 1822; George III die-stamped shovel, ivory handle, Joseph Wilmore, 1818; George III plain shovel, mother-of-pearl handle, Samuel Pemberton, 1804.

12. Miscellaneous caddy spoons, centre, William IV rococo die-stamped leaf, George Unite, 1834; Left to right: George III superbly shaped elongated leaf, bright-cut handle, Thomas Wallis, London, 1800; George III grape-and-vine leaf by Matthew Linwood, Birmingham, 1819; George III pierced bowl, George Baskerville, London 1796; George III ribbed leaf, tendril handle, Wardell and Kempson, Birmingham, 1816; Victorian silver-gilt floral rococo leaf, cast finial, Hilliard and Thomasson, Birmingham. 1852.

13. Leaf caddy spoon with finely chased veins and stalk handle, Birmingham, c. 1800.

14. Jockey-cap spoon, Birmingham, c. 1805.

15. This globular George II tea kettle made by John Swift is typical of those popular around the third decade of the 18th century. The ebony handle matches the simple knob of the lid. (Sotheby)

decided on the uncompromising, rounded base, at the same time equipping it with a stand.

Neo-classical design played a major role in the work of American silversmiths, and much elegant silver was produced during this period, including some outstanding New York pieces, characterised by excellent bright-cutting. This technique had become highly developed in Birmingham. Craftsmen used a specially designed gouge (in various sizes) to cut narrow channels, slanting these in various directions, to give a faceted effect. Much beautiful bright-cutting is still to be found on pieces today.

Although the rolling-mill had been in use for many years, during the last two or three decades of the 18th century it played an ever-increasing part in the production of silver, and to cut costs was used to roll silver to even finer gauges. This thin silver was ideal for automatic stamping-out of shapes. Whole sections of a tea pot could be produced in this way, then joined by almost invisible soldering. The speed at which decoration was automatically added grew to match that of the speedy stamping-out process.

Generally, decorative effects were added in various ways. The silver might be stamped in low relief, between appropriately sunk dies, or it might be cut in a variety of open-work patterns, achieved by varying the punches. In early work this press-stamped piercing was used as the background for relief motifs which were then soldered on. Later, techniques had so improved that most of these were incorporated in the actual press-cut design. During the last decade or so of the 18th century, a harder steel was developed, which meant that the tool contained in the fly-press lost its precision less rapidly, and thus was able to complete more runs and more complicated patterns.

Despite these factory techniques which meant that many more people were able to avail themselves of silver, master silversmiths were still patronised by the wealthy. They continued with their original method of hammering up from the flat, and hand decorating with engraving or chasing. Collectors may detect a hand-raised piece by looking inside for the old hammer marks.

Towards the turn of the 19th century, designs in tea pots had become amazingly diverse. There was something to suit many pockets, if not in silver, then certainly in Sheffield plate. Already by 1770, Matthew Boulton and his partner John Fothergill had equipped their Soho, Birmingham, factory specially for manu-facturing component parts. These were then sold to other firms for assembling and final finishing.

Meanwhile, the neo-classical period was drawing to its final stages, to be replaced by the romance and splendour of the Regency era. One of the great Regency silversmiths was Paul Storr (working 1792–1821) who had been apprenticed to Fogel-berg. From Fogelberg's workshop in Church Street had come some exceptional and original neo-classical silver. Paul Storr's work was greatly influenced by Fogelberg.

The urn-shaped tea pot, elegant on its stem and well-balanced foot, was popular both here and in America, and while this style and others influenced by Adam lingered on, the new designs rapidly gained in popularity. These were square, polygonal, oval or circular, their sides usually curving upwards and culminating outwards towards an angular shoulder. Lids were flat, domed or moulded. Handles were of ivory, wood or silver, with insulating material inserted. These were commonly of rectangular section with a flat top. The bases were as diverse as the pots, sometimes low moulded, or with low stems, with three or four ball feet. One popular shape copied extensively in ceramics has a peaked front.

Ornament was often lacking completely, but when it was used, it included embossed or applied gadrooning, the ever popular form of decoration, imitation rococo embossing, and, for once, an idea taken from the potter rather than the reverse, that of the repetitive branch patterns which were inspired by the Wedgwood borders.

Numbers of tea services now began to appear, no doubt as a result of the greater imports of tea. They usually consisted of a tea pot, milk jug, sugar bowl and matching hot-water jug, with an occasional additional item being a kettle on a stand. It was not uncommon for the jug to be mounted on a tripod stand with a spirit burner below. Combined tea and coffee sets were also quite usual.

American silversmiths from Philadelphia, New York, Boston and the smaller centres, were by now producing a wide variety of beautiful pieces for the tea table. Superlative of its kind is the tea set by Revere, circa 1792, in the Minneapolis Institute of Arts, which was made for John Templeman of Boston, and is the only

Revere tea set known to be complete. As with contemporary English examples, the tea pot has a stand on four feet, to protect the table surface. Elegant fluting is used on all the pieces which include a cream jug, sugar urn and caddy. The latter, to match the tea pot, has an identical stand. There is as well a strainer, a delightful shell-shaped caddy spoon and sugar tongs. Delicate bright-cutting of classical motifs is used throughout.

Whereas neo-classical designs were inspired by Greco-Roman styles, Regency ornament was derived from Imperial Rome, ancient Egypt and the Far and Near East. Thus heavier and far more opulent decoration now succeeded the clean, flowing styles influenced by Adam. Regency ornament was characterised by motifs of numerous ancient origins, which were usually quite well produced. They were used concurrently with rococo ornament which was undergoing a revival, embracing the usual C and S scrolls, shells and flowers, generally flat-chased or applied. The work which was produced during this revival cannot really be compared with the 18th century rococo, lacking as it did the inspiration of the earlier work, and becoming far heavier generally. There are, none the less, some examples of merit. During this period and later, silver tea pots or other items of tea equipage might be sent away to the silversmith to be decorated in the revised rococo style. Such pieces are not always spotted by new collectors, who should beware of buying heavily decorated objects unless they are quite sure such decoration is contemporary.

Outstanding artists of the period like John Flaxman, Francis Chantrey and William Theed, influenced styles both here and in America. American silver incorporates most of the main English features.

The Industrial Revolution in both countries ultimately led to a decline in the standards which had been the pride of craftsmen down the centuries. Out of this diminishing quality, however, evolved new methods of manufacture like electro-plating and cheaper forms of Sheffield plating, both of which are discussed in the relevant chapters.

CHAPTER TWO

CADDIES AND CADDY SPOONS

"Tea, although an Oriental,
Is a gentleman at least;
Cocoa is a cad and coward,
Cocoa is a vulgar beast."

G. K. Chesterton

Certainly tea has always retained an element of gentility. In the
18th century, despite the growing addiction for it by those who
could scarce afford such an indulgence, the association of tea with
the more gracious social ritual was as pronounced as ever. Its cult
among the fashionable was lessened not at all by its growing
popularity with the masses, and in the great houses of the land tea
drinking continued amidst the splendour of lavish furnishings and
silver, rivalled only in enthusiasm by the ordinary man brewing
his tea in a modest earthenware pot.

An extravagant use of silver had been apparent since the days
of Charles II, and it was customary for the upper strata of society
to acquire silver as an appropriate display of wealth and substance.
It was, therefore, natural that silver should also be used for early
tea cups, and it is thought that these probably appeared towards
the end of the seventeenth century. Needless to say, their popularity was apparently short-lived, due among other things to the
excellent heat-conduction qualities of the metal and the fact that
these early cups had no handles. It must have been quite a painful
operation taking tea from such vessels. Nevertheless, no book on
tea equipage would be complete without a mention of them, even
though they are extremely rare today, probably because most
would have been melted down when cups of porcelain became
more readily available. Such examples that do exist, as the one

36

shown in this book (see plate No. 9), were very simple objects, purely functional in design, mostly with little elegance of form. Others might have matching silver stands, and one specimen even has two handles. A handleless cup and saucer can be seen at the Victoria and Albert Museum.

Domestic tea canisters appeared towards the end of the 17th century. In one form or another they have been with us ever since. It is thought that early examples derived their shape from the oriental stoppered jar of porcelain, their undecorated sides usually rising from a rectangular base, curving in at the shoulders to a circular neck which was fitted with a separate high-domed cover or lid. These separate covers were probably used to measure the required quantity of tea. In later examples the top section, including the neck, sometimes slid off; in others there was a sliding panel fitted in the base.

An early example of 1699 which can be seen at the Ashmolean Museum, Oxford, is practically an exact cube of 8 cms (3⅛ inches) with panels on each side and a circular slip-on cap. More common during Queen Anne's reign, and later, were the taller variety, rectangular, octangular or hexagonal, sometimes triangular, on a moulded base with a hinged domed cap. Decoration consisted mostly of horizontal mouldings. They were commonly made in sets of two, for green and black tea respectively; and also in sets of three, the third being for another tea or for sugar. All would be contained in an outer case which might be covered in a variety of materials including leather, shagreen, tortoiseshell and mother-of-pearl. A lock would be fitted to this outer case as a fitting precaution at a time when tea was so expensive. Canisters were also made as individual pieces, or complemented the various styles of current tea pot designs. During the 18th century an amazing array of shapes, with an equally wide variety of ornament appeared. Sometimes, as with the earlier examples, these would be simple and well proportioned. Later canisters might be decorated with embossing of rococo or Chinese ornament.

In America only a few canisters have survived from the Queen Anne period, and these are generally from New York. An example by Simeon Soumain in the Metropolitan Museum of Art, New York, follows its current English counterpart exactly, being octagonal in form with a high-domed cover. It bears the Buyard arms in an ornamental cartouche.

The word caddy was not commonly adopted in England until the later years of the 18th century, and is thought to have come from the word catty (kati), a weight used in China, equal to a little over one pound avoirdupois.

The dome-necked canister remained popular until well into the second half of the 18th century, although other designs, basically similar, were also being made concurrently. A rectangular box with a stepped lid to complement, or sometimes to match, the applied foot-rim which was built in tiers of moulding, was a common alternative. Lid and rim mouldings would be produced from strips of hand-worked silver. Towards the middle of the century, decoration chased in bold relief over the top of the body became more common, and by about 1750 the *bombé* outline then so fashionable on commodes of the period was echoed in the shape of some canisters which took on ogee outlines, curving in at a low waist and out again at top and bottom. They might stand on dainty feet shaped as acanthus leaves or some other popular motif of the period. The lids were slightly domed, and often topped by a cast finial in the shape of a shell or pineapple. In common with tea pots, the covers might also be surmounted by a Chinaman, standing out in full relief against an ornate background of scrolls, shells, rockwork and general asymmetry.

Other outlines during the third decade or so of the 18th century resembled oriental vases. These attractive canisters were decorated with flower designs and flowing scrolls worked in repoussé on current items of tea equipage. How dissimilar they were to the simple little bottle-neck canisters common during the early years of the century. The swirling, imaginative rococo decoration remained in fashion until the late years of the 1760's, when it was supplanted in popularity by neo-classical styles.

Canisters were now larger and contained probably twice as much tea as their predecessors, whose small dimensions were only big enough for about 115 to 170 grammes (four to six ounces). The introduction of factory-type silversmithing and changes in techniques which coincided with the arrival of the neo-classical period, meant that caddies could be produced in a wide variety of shapes at less cost. Typical of the period was the outline based on an Adam vase or urn. The elegant, tapering body was embossed in low relief with an array of classical decoration, flowers or convex flutes. The graceful, incurving shoulders culminated in a domed cover, which shortly became concave in outline. Sometimes ring handles were added. These remained popular until the first two decades or so of the 19th century.

Also greatly favoured was the simple box-shaped caddy. Although far plainer in outline, these boxes with vertical sides and flat tops, square, rectangular or hexagonal, possessed much charm of their own. They might be exquisitely bright-cut with neo-classical motifs, their flat lids decorated with a cast knob. From about the last two decades of the 18th century this knob would commonly be in the shape of the pineapple. Some lids were hinged, enabling them to be fitted with a lock. Other caddies would be chased or engraved, or with some quite simple form of decoration like gadrooning. Caddies in two's or three's might be contained in wooden chests. A further design consisted of two separate lidded compartments, with an additional lid over these. With the revival of the rococo style in the 19th century, caddies took on more exaggerated ornament. What they lacked in 18th century charm, they made up for in a profusion of decoration.

American tea caddies were made in greater quantity during the neo-classical period than probably any other. The oval shape was general, and bright-cutting was one of the most popular forms of decoration. Sometimes it is used excessively. During this period generally, American silversmiths produced a rich variety of tea silver, much being of the highest calibre. Ornate, but very beautiful, is the fine caddy by Daniel van Voorhis (New York Historical Society), decorated with garlands of flowers over the body and classical motifs around the base and top. The lid is hinged and fitted with a lock.

Some caddies might also be equipped with their own stands, as in the case of the superb example by Andrew Fogelberg and S. Gilbert, circa 1876, which matches the tea pot and stand described in Chapter One, which can be seen at the Victoria and Albert Museum. American caddies might also have a stand, possibly to match a tea pot and stand in a tea set.

By the second decade of the 19th century, caddies, like all other pieces of domestic silver, reflected the florid styles already mentioned. The established habit of tea drinking had ensured their continued role in the homes of successive generations, and rendered them an indispensable item of tea equipage.

CADDY SPOONS

The growing popularity of tea during the 18th century meant that it began to attract attention as a worthwhile source of government revenue. As early as 1695 a tax of one shilling in the pound was placed on tea which was imported lawfully (i.e. that which arrived in ships of the East India Company) and half as much again, 1s 6d on unlawful cargoes. This was doubled in 1704, and only eight years later a further increase was imposed. To make life easier for itself, the government gave the monopoly of tea importation to the East India Company (not only for England, but also America) so that all taxes could be collected from one source. In 1747 the tax was again increased and not surprisingly imports decreased. It was finally decided some twenty years later to suspend the tax of one shilling in the pound for five years on black and Singlo teas (green tea) to increase consumption at home and to encourage export to Ireland and the American colonies. The result was an increase of over six million pounds in England and Wales. Pitt, by his Commutation Act of 1784 reduced the high duties, replacing the tax by a flat twelve and a half per cent of the value at import. Moreover, he placed a legal obligation on the East India Company to import enough tea into England to satisfy the demand without raising the price.

This abundance of tea was an important contributing factor to the enormous upsurge in the demand for tea equipage generally, as well as influencing the development of another, small tea-time utensil, which was to become one of the most popular and mass-produced of all the pieces, namely the charming little caddy spoon.

In early tea canisters, the domed lid was usually utilised to measure the amount of tea required. But when hinged lids took their place, some sort of ladle became necessary. Originally this might take the form of a deep bowl with a more or less vertical handle. Sometimes a hook would be placed at the rear of the handle in order to hang it in the tea chest. Gradually, the vertical handle gave way to the shorter stem we usually associate with the caddy spoon, and because of their decrease in size it became the custom to keep these, as they are today, in the caddy together with the tea. Although only a small number were made before about 1770, after this time their output grew increasingly. When Pitt obligated the East India Company to satisfy the tea demands of the country without raising the price, tea drinking became the sempiternal habit of the British, and with it came a corresponding demand for caddy spoons. Most could afford the small price of a silver caddy spoon which could be used with any type of caddy, be it Sheffield plate, ceramic or silver. By the end of the century, Birmingham silversmiths, who specialised in smaller objects, had become prolific in their output of the little spoons, which they continued to be for the next fifty years or more.

Although the Act of 1790 exempted from hall-marking smaller objects which weighed less than five pennyweights, caddy spoons were among the items named specifically as being excluded from this concession, with the exception of filigree work. All caddy spoons should therefore bear hall-marks.

A wonderful variety of these diminutive ladles now began to appear on the market. They were made by two main methods. Sometimes the ladle bowl was die struck and the handle pressed, the handle and bowl then being joined by hand. Others were stamped in a single piece. From about the second decade of the 19th century very ornate examples were cast. The bowls of very early caddy spoons were usually hammered up from the flat by hand from a sheet of silver, but cast specimens were also produced.

Caddy spoons have long delighted collectors, and it is not difficult to see why. At their best they are superb examples of the quality of work which late 18th century craftsmen were well able to produce. Their variety alone leaves one amazed at the ingenuity of their makers; their decoration has a singular charm of its own; and their diminutive, delicate characteristic adds to their general appeal. They might be embossed, chased, engraved, bright-cut, fluted or left quite plain. Sadly, many of the fragile early examples often suffered breakages where the stem joins the bowl. Thus, many have been repaired through the years, and it is as well to check them at this point.

A very popular shape was that of the jockey cap, the inside of the cap being the ladle, and the visor the handle. Many of these were produced, and on some the hall-marks and duty mark appear on the visor, while other examples are marked elsewhere, usually at the back of the cap, or inside the crown. The more common type of jockey-cap caddy spoon includes those with a plain, seg-mented cap which is usually engraved and bright-cut on the peak; a 'ribbed' cap and peak; and a die-stamped type decorated with geometric patterns. Some jockey caps were also made in silver filigree or simulated filigree.

Another very popular design was the vine leaf, with a bunch of grapes embossed in the centre, the handle being a vine tendril. There was also a tea leaf with chased veins, the handle being a curled stalk; a cast strawberry leaf with a twisted tendril handle; and a stirrup design.

Quite rare are the eagle caddy spoons sought after by collectors. Made from one piece of silver, the handle is the bird's neck which terminates in a hooked beak, while the bowl is delicately formed into plumage. Georgian examples date from the end of the 18th century, but they continued to be made as late as 1840, although these may not be considered of so great a merit as early examples. There are also examples produced in the 1850's. The hall-marks appear in various places, perhaps in the repoussé feathers, or on the back of the bowl or the handle.

At the beginning of the 19th century, and continuing for the first fifteen years or so, war trophies were fashionable, including a standard, pennon, cannon, drum, fife, bayonet and sword. The bowl of the spoon would be embossed with one or other of these, and sometimes the handle would bear the name of a victory.

A further design was the hand-shaped caddy spoon. The bowl was the hand, and the handle was the flat wrist, often giving the impression of a lace cuff, being decorated with bright-cutting, or perhaps with a monogram.

Other shapes included the shell-shaped bowl; various types in filigree or simulated filigree which was die-struck; scoops and shovels; acorns and thistles. Many were of no particular shape, but relied instead on bright-cutting for distinction. This might appear on both the handle and bowl, or on just the bowl. Some had handles of ebony or stained boxwood.

Although most caddy spoons came from Birmingham and thus

bear the Birmingham assay mark of an anchor, others also emitted from Sheffield, London, York, Exeter, Chester and Glasgow. Irish specimens tended to be larger; perhaps the Irish liked their tea stronger. However, it was the Birmingham silversmiths who really excelled at this little spoon, and whose productivity was prolific in the extreme.

The Birmingham assay office was not, in fact, opened until 1773, and until then all silver had to be sent to either London or Chester for hall-marking. This state of affairs got rapidly out of hand with the increase in production of all types of silver, and as is described in the chapter on hall-marks, Matthew Boulton petitioned Parliament to end the laborious trips across country with heavy and valuable loads of silver. However, Birmingham never rivalled London in the production of domestic plate and the more important pieces, as examples of every conceivable type of silver, have been assayed in London for generations.

Caddy spoons made towards the end of the 18th century and for the first few years of the 19th century are the most delicate of all. Generally speaking later 19th century examples tended to be heavier and more ornate, one example being an overpowering lady in a crinoline holding a parasol, the bowl being formed as a chased rococo shell. This was made in 1841 and others with figures for the handles were produced at about the same time. They really bore little resemblance to the fragile 18th century specimen, but reflected instead the obsessive love of decoration so characteristic of the Victorians.

CHAPTER THREE

TEA KETTLES AND URNS

*"Tea! thou soft, thou sober, sage, and venerable
liquid . . . wink-tipling cordial, to whose glorious
insipidity I owe the happiest moments of my life,
let me fall prostrate."*

Colley Cibber

The tea kettle played a prominent role in the early story of tea equipage. Gradually it became almost synonymous with the tea ritual itself, occupying as the kettle did so splendid a place over the rest of the silver. Certainly its rotund form aglow in the flickering firelight must have cheered many a soul on a bleak winter's afternoon. From its early days the kettle had always occupied a place of importance, the plump, homely shape reflecting the simplicity of line of the early tea pot. However, only a few decades were to pass before the kettle, shrouded in the glories of rococo decoration, resplendent with all manner of ornament, positively dominated the entire scene.

Records prove that the tea kettle had made its first appearance towards the end of the 17th century, although few examples of this not very elegant species survive with hall-marks earlier than about the first few years of the 18th century. The kettle, or some other handy means of heating the water, was a natural development. Early tea pots were usually of such small proportions that they required constant replenishing, thus the kettle was the practical solution. Queen Anne tea kettles usually had a bun-shaped form, based on the pear-shaped tea pot. Despite the uncompromisingly bulgy outline of these, what they lacked in elegance they made up for in a certain prosaic charm. A grooved band usually encircled the shoulders, while the rims were additionally strengthened with narrow moulding. The spouts, however, brought welcome relief to this utilitarian vessel. This was commonly of the elegant swan-neck variety, sometimes with its base faceted and its tip incorporating a hinged cover. Further slight appeasement to the eye came with the minaret lid and its knob of ebony or stained black wood. The handle was of the swing variety, with a hand-grip made of either of the materials used for the knobs, which it would match. These earlier tea kettles were usually provided with a lamp and stand; the latter consisting of either a plain or pierced ring, fitting the base of the kettle which was quite flat. The stand stood upon three legs, from which curved horizontal branches to a small ring supporting the spirit lamp. The wick would be covered by a hinged dome. Sometimes a pair of lamp-snuffers might hang on the rim of the stand. There might also be two hinged handles on the ring of the stand so that a servant might carry the whole apparatus, plus the filled kettle, to the mistress of the house.

An early American kettle by Cornelius Kierstede in the Metropolitan Museum of Art, New York, closely resembles the English bun-shaped kettle, except that it is slightly less rotund, and its swan-neck spout more elaborate. Its handle-grip is of dyed wood, and the lid is domed, neatly surmounted by an elongated finial.

Thus, the tea kettle bore a close resemblance to the shape of the tea pot, and when the latter became several-sided in plan, the kettle followed suit. In these cases the rotund form seems to take on a newly found elegance, its eight- or twelve-sided outline having an elongated effect. Not only did kettles closely resemble tea pots; some were exact replicas, simply enlarged to suit their function. On this variety, the swing handle would be replaced by a vertical scroll-shaped tea-pot type of handle, made of wood. During this period the legs which supported the stand were generally in inverted baluster form. Occasionally, the lifting handles of the stand might be replaced by a straight handle of wood or ivory. By the early years of the second decade of the 18th century the lifting handles disappeared altogether, and at the same time the spirit container increased in capacity. In some cases it might almost reach down as far as the table surface. Sometimes the tea kettle took pride of place on its own separate silver tripod table. Such tables stood about 76 cms (30 inches) high, and were carefully placed by a servant in a strategic position. They had elegant baluster stems upon which was a table top usually resembling a salver of contemporary design. Instead of this there might be a ring top, containing the spirit lamp, in which the base of the kettle would safely rest. With some tray-top tables, the tray might sometimes only be screwed on, so that it could be used separately as a tray. In the case of the ring top, the lamp was usually part of the stand.

In addition to the pear-shaped kettle, there was a globular shape which was usually used in conjunction with the small, globular tea pot of the period. This kettle became fashionable around the third decade of the 18th century, continuing in popularity for several years. Its lid differed from earlier kettles, in that this now followed the general outline, instead of surmounting it. The ivory or ebony knob on the lid matched the handle-grip. Sometimes the bow-shaped grip might be bound with cane. Alternatively it could be of wood as in early examples. This kettle was less heavy in weight than its predecessor, and its globular shape automatically meant a narrowing in at the base, which had to be strengthened for stability and a small moulded foot-rim added.

Until about the third decade of the 18th century, the kettle had remained comparatively undecorated, following the ornamental simplicity of the period. Now it began to reflect a reversal of this purity. The rococo influence was to become more apparent on the tea kettle than probably any other piece of tea equipage, completely transforming this homely vessel into dominant magnificence, entirely contrasting with its former modesty.

Now it became a piece of rococo extravaganza; often lavish in its decoration; sometimes almost fantastic; but hardly ever mundane. Occasionally it might be described as positively regal, embossed as it could be with an incredible miscellanea of ornament, including sprays of flowers, foliage patterns, twirling scroll work and pouting cherubs. Such a medley of decoration might be carried through to the spout which had become as elaborate as the remainder of the vessel, handsomely chased and decorated.

Neither was the tripod stand excluded from these rococo frivolities. The legs of this might bear all manner of ornament, and even the lamp ring did not go unadorned. It, too, was enveloped in ornate moulding. Sometimes the tripod stand was equipped with an elegant tray which stood upon decorated feet. In others, the spirit-lamp was protected from draughts by a panelled and perforated silver wind shield. The stand might also have a pair of silver pegs attached to guard chains. These fitted into holes drilled through the foot-rim of the kettle and the kettle rim of the stand, in order that the kettle, stand and lamp could all be carried by the kettle handle.

Many of these elaborately decorated kettles were produced from thin silver, yet despite this they were expensive because of the amount of work which went into their decoration. Many could not afford the luxury of such ornament, and because of this quite plain kettles were produced concurrently during the rococo period, with perhaps a little flat chasing as decoration. Arms in asymmetrical cartouches might also be engraved.

One of the earliest complete examples of American globular tea kettles, which still has its stand, is by Jacob Hurd and is engraved with the Lowell arms. This is very simple and elegant. It has little decoration, except for the elaborate cartouche and faceted, swan-neck spout. The handle is slender and delicate. The overall simplicity is emphasised by the ornate legs of the stand which are a graceful cabriole shape, sparingly decorated with naturalistic motifs, reaching to the claw feet.

A truly splendid example of American rococo silver is the tea kettle and stand by the Philadelphian silversmith Joseph Richardson. This magnificent vessel weighs over 2·5 kilograms (90 ounces), and, it is thought, was inspired by a kettle ordered from the London Huguenot silversmith Paul de Lamerie in 1744 by the Franks family in Philadelphia. Its inverted pear-shaped body has a narrow foot-rim fitted into the ring of the stand, which is upon three scroll legs with shell feet. Between the legs hang festoons of cast decoration incorporating pierced shells, foliage and other naturalistic forms, and these are repeated in the chasing or repoussé on the elaborate cartouche which surrounds the Plumstead arms. The light curved spout culminates in a bird's head and is embellished with further rococo decoration, while the exquisite scrolls of the swing-handle not only stand out in fine silhouette but balance perfectly the scroll-shaped legs, set delicately on shell feet. The ornate lid is gently domed and is surmounted by a cast silver pineapple.

47

An English example of extreme rococo decoration was made by Charles Kandler about fifteen years before the date of the Richardson kettle, 1727–1737. This is certainly even more fantastic. Superbly and heavily embossed with marine mythological figures, its spout is a demi-triton blowing a conch; its finial a cherubic boy; while the two arms of its swing-handle are composed of slender mermaids in somewhat abandoned poses. This marine fantasy is supported by a stand which incorporates silver pegs attached to guard chains, as already described, so that the whole piece of equipage could be carried by the kettle handle.

Towards the middle of the 18th century, the kettle intended for the fashionable London home took on the graceful ogee shape. Lids were still flat, so that the general outline was quite uninterrupted, and the body was lavishly decorated with all manner of rococo chased and embossed motifs. By about 1750 the lid had developed into a dome shape, topped with a popular form of finial. The spout was likewise decorated with scroll work and naturalistic ornament, terminating in a bird's head. Towards the end of the 1750's the kettle opening was raised into a gadrooned rim, and a flat-domed lid fitted into this.

Tea kettles continued to be fashionable for the following fifteen years or so. Gradually their popularity declined, however, until by about 1775 the tea urn had practically superseded them. During the last phase of their popularity, there had been ever growing demands for a bigger type of kettle. This had led to the development of a rather ungainly vessel with a far larger capacity which entirely eliminated the graceful spout, replacing it with a functional ball-handled tap, positioned at the bottom of the vessel above the base. The advantage of this innovation was that there was no longer any need for the vessel to be tilted when pouring; the hostess simply turned the tap. Nevertheless, it was ugly in outline, with ill-proportioned sloping sides and a wide cane-covered handle. The body was supported on a frame of four curved and reeded legs, with the lamp between them. This half-way vessel evolved into the tea urn.

TEA URNS

The most popular form of tea urn was based on the vase shape. It stood elegantly on a stemmed foot, and presented a pleasant change after the ungainly in-between vessel already mentioned. The type which had no lamp kept the water hot by an entirely different method, a red-hot cylindrical box-iron, which was inserted into a silver socket contained within the body of the urn. The water circulated around this and thus retained its heat. By the turn of the 19th century, this socket was usually contained in the centre of the urn.

Another method was by charcoal. The body of the urn when removed from the base revealed a round and perforated silver container, into which the hot charcoal would be tipped. Sometimes this might also be made of some other type of metal. The resultant hot air then travelled through a tube, usually of copper, which rose through the urn before finally emerging at a loose finial surmounting the lid. This finial was removed to cause a draught to hasten combustion and draw heat through the tube. The circulating water around the hot tube thus retained its heat.

It is commonly thought that the lamp-heated urns were used for drawing off tea into cups, while the red-hot iron and charcoal variety were purely for hot water.

The tea urn of the slender, classical vase shape, however, which became extremely popular during the hey-day of the neo-classical period, was not only well received in England. It was a shape much favoured by American silversmiths, and one of the first neo-classical pieces to be made in America, two years before the Revolution, was a tea urn by Richard Humphreys of Philadelphia in this shape. It was given by members of the first Constitutional Congress to its secretary, Charles Thomson, in 1774, and reflects most English characteristics of the period. Instead of the usual curving or recurving handles, it has an unusual angular, square shape, however, which hardly complements the flowing lines of the classical urn form. They tend to create a discordant effect on the entire shoulder line. Bands of beading encircle the cover, base and foot of the stem, and vertical acanthus leaf motifs embellish the base of the body. Apart from this, and a decorative border on the square foot and beneath the shoulders of the urn, there is little other decoration except for the delicate, engraved cartouche around the inscription.

Generally speaking the classical tall, vase-shaped urn was usually lacking in ornament. Its graceful outline could well stand alone without such embellishment as most silversmiths were quick to discover. However, it became enhanced by a pair of recurving handles which swept upwards towards the lid and then down to the slender, tapering base. This type of handle became common both in England and America.

A fine example by the Boston silversmith Paul Revere, made around 1800, is perfect in its simplicity, bearing only the minimum of decoration, and this in the form of bright-cut floral borders beneath the shoulders and on the top and lid. The handles are of the recurving variety and the square foot-rim is set upon ball-and-claw feet.

During the last decade of the 18th century, the narrow neck of this style of urn was broadened, and human or animal heads with pendant rings were added as handles. Similarly, the tap became ornate and might also be in the shape of a head of an animal or bird. Four columns with claw feet, standing on a flat base, often supported the urn which had remained lamp-heated. The spirit-lamp itself might be in the form of a small urn.

Earlier lampless tea urns had a squat, pear-shaped body. They might be embossed with plain or foliated scrolls and given a cartouche. Lids were usually bell-shaped with a knob shaped in the form of a popular design. Scroll handles were attached, and the moulded silver spout might be embellished with classical motifs. Thumb-pieces were often of ebony or green-stained ivory as was the insulating material used in the handles. The base of the body stood upon a high stem which was supported by a square plinth. Gadrooning might decorate the former, piercing the latter. Four feet supported the plinth.

The tea urn with a ball-shaped body became popular towards the end of the century. This was either quite plain or perhaps might be fluted. A few years after the turn of the century the shape of the wider vase became fashionable. This evolved and gradually merged with that of the ball-shaped body, the body becoming quite hemispherical. Beneath the body a stemmed foot rose from a square base mounted on four legs.

After about the first decade of the century the body rim became everted and decoration, often incorporating wide fluting, embellished the lower portion. There were numerous urns of this type, some appearing to possess two lid rims, each decorated with some form of moulding. Various mounts and finials now appeared which were used quite indiscriminately; there was little coherence in decoration generally.

Tea turns made during the first two or three decades or so of the 19th century appeared in all shapes and guises, but like much of the silver of the period they lacked the elegance of their predecessors. Although described as revived rococo, the description is debatable.

Outstanding among the pieces made in America at this time is a large tea urn by Forbes and Son, and presented by the Firemen of the City of New York to their trustee, John W. Degraux in 1835. All manner of naturalistic rococo motifs envelop the lid and the circular base rim and entwine the handles. In fact, the whole encrusted vessel leaves the eye in a total state of visual bewilderment.

Towards the turn of the 19th century another rather more elaborate specimen had appeared. This was the apparatus known as the tea and coffee machine, which was made from about 1790. It consisted of tea, coffee and water containers and sometimes a slop basin. The basic design was utilitarian in the extreme, and the whole effect completely lacking in any sort of aesthetic appeal. It was simply a central urn for hot water, usually twice as big as a tea and coffee urn which were positioned either side of it. The more capacious central urn swivelled on its base, so that the smaller ones could be quickly filled without moving them. The three urns were usually portable and could thus also be used separately. The water would be heated by a hot iron or a spirit lamp, and the trio generally stood on a platform on four feet.

CHAPTER FOUR

SPOONS

"When the tea is brought at five o'clock,
And all the neat curtains are drawn with care,
The little black cat with bright green eyes
Is suddenly purring there."

Harold Monroe

Silver spoons have a history which can be traced back to the Middle Ages. They were used by the wealthy few for general eating purposes, and did not become the refined, specific utensils that we know for hundreds of years. As far as collecting is concerned, spoons probably have the widest appeal of all items connected with tea equipage. Although rare and early spoons can be collected at great expense, later examples can be acquired for quite modest sums and collected individually or gradually to form part of a set based on a certain style. Spoons have an important and interesting history, and because of this all collectors should know something about their evolution over the years.

At one time the silver spoon was a much prized possession. Anybody lucky enough to own one made a point of seeing that this was bequeathed to a cherished kinsman in his will. Records as early as the 14th century reveal that spoons were itemised in wills.

The spoon maker, or spooner as he was also called, was thus among the most ancient of our craftsmen. He originally fashioned his spoons from horn, wood or metal. Gold and silver were used only for ecclesiastical spoons. It was not until the 13th century that the silver spoon began to make an appearance on the domestic scene, and this was only in the homes of a very few. By the 14th century they had become slightly more common, but were still looked upon as something very special. Their owners guarded them carefully, ensuring that they were always replaced in their tooled leather cases. While there are examples of very early spoons, these are mostly in museums. Silver dealers of high calibre also have them from time to time.

Until about the middle of the 17th century, these crude utensils would be hammered into shape from a single piece of silver. An ornamental knop of some popular cast shape would be soldered into a notch at the end of the stem. Sometimes such knops would be of silver, while other spoons might have gilt examples. The average length of a spoon would be 15 to 18 cms (6 or 7 inches), which was ideal for the function they performed, not of stirring, but of spooning up food. Certain soft foods were actually called spoon-meat until well into the 17th century. Because the bowls of early spoons tended to be shallow, they were hardly appropriate for liquids, and suitable bowls were gradually developed for this purpose. The outline of the stems also evolved. Very early stems were diamond-shaped in section, tapering a little towards the finial. A later type was hexagonal and also tapered towards the knop.

The knop finials which add so much charm and character to these early spoons embrace no more than about twelve basic designs, apart from those taken from family crests or specifically ordered by customers. Among the usual finials are the diamond point, the acorn, the moor's head, wrythen (a ball marked with spiral twistings), hexagonal, woodwose (wildman with a club), ball, lion sejant and seal top. The maidenhead finial was also popular, and although spoons with these knops are particularly common during the 16th century, mention has been made of them in far earlier wills. The Virgin Mary is the source of inspiration for the maidenhead spoon. In very early spoons the head which formed the knop quite often bore the horned headdress popular during the first fifty years or so of the 15th century. Later coiffures appear on successive knops. These spoons were also bequeathed in wills, as were apostle spoons, the knops of which took the shape of one of the twelve apostles, and of Christ in majesty, to make a complete set of thirteen. Such spoons were bought single and in sets, and were a customary Christening present, the child being given the spoon bearing his saint's name.

It is useful to know how to detect each saint, as although these spoons are very expensive, one can sometimes find later reproductions at realistic prices. They include: St. Peter, a key, two keys or a fish; St. John, a chalice, eagle or palm branch; St. Andrew, a saltire cross; St. James the Greater, a staff and other pilgrim characteristics; St. James the Less, a Fuller's bat, because he was killed by a blow on the head from Simeon the Fuller; St. Phillip, a pastoral staff, and perhaps a basket of bread; St. Bartholomew, a butcher's knife; St. Simon Zelotes, a long saw; St. Thomas, a spear; St. Jude, a cross or club; St. Matthias, an axe or lance; St. Matthew, a wallet, sometimes an axe; St. Paul, a sword.

Seal-top spoons were also typical of the period, and continued so to be well into the second half of the 17th century. The stems of these were topped with a flat disc shape which might be closely pricked with the initials or monogram of the owner. Sometimes there might be a date instead.

The slipped-in-the-stalk spoon, the stem of which did not end in the usual sort of knop finial came well into fashion during the first half of the 17th century, although this type of spoon had been made in moderation well before this date. Its increase in popularity marked an important stage in the development of the spoon. For the first time, the stem devoid of its ornamental finial began to resemble the spoon as we know it today. The end of this stem terminated in a slant, shaped from the front of the spoon. Very early examples had slender stems, but these were lengthened and broadened in later examples. Sometimes the owner's initials might be impressed on the bowl or pricked upon the slipped end.

The earliest type of spoon known to have been made in America is this slipped-in-the-stalk variety, a fine example of which, by the Boston silversmith Jeremiah Dummer, is at Yale University Art Gallery. In New York it became the custom to give a spoon to pallbearers at funerals, and these would be marked with the name and age of the deceased, together with the date. Such spoons are quite distinctive with Dutch characteristics and ornate, complicated stems.

From the simple slip-in-the-stalk variety developed the stump end, which marked a further important stage in the design of the spoon, its faceted, sided stem tapered to more of a point, and looking just a little more like a modern spoon. By about 1650 this had evolved into what came to be known as the Puritan spoon, the stem of which was cut squarely off at the end. The bowl of this spoon was an oval shape, and the stem joined it in a V-shape.

These spoons really laid the foundation of the general form which all future spoons were basically to follow. They marked a complete turning point in the development of the stem, eliminating as they did the ornamental knop finial, so beloved by preceding generations, and terminating instead with some sort of flat decoration, or later, irregularity of outline.

Gradually the plain end of the Puritan spoon, uncompromising and severe, gave way to a more decorative shape. The simple square was hammered out into a thin blade, leaf shape, which was cut vertically with two deep notches near to the sides, thus dividing it into three sections and forming a simple trefoil, two smaller lobes flanking the main central one. These spoons came to be known as trefid (trifid). Later examples usually have almost equal lobes. The hammered, almost symmetrical oval bowl and stem were strengthened at the back by a tapering rib which ran from the junction of the two parts, and these were the forerunners of the elongated tapered wedge of rat-tail spoons which became common during successive decades.

Sometimes these spoons were plain, but they might also be engraved with a foliage pattern up the stem. On others the back of the bowl would bear decoration, usually with a pattern known as lace work, the rat-tail being integrated into the design. Later spoons had both their stems and the backs of the bowls covered in a scroll-work pattern.

An American spoon by John Coney is typical of the English influence in this scroll decoration, with scroll work on the back of the bowl, and the initials of the owner engraved on the back of the stem, this being quite usual in both England and America.

There were generally two main sizes of trefids, a small one about 16·5 cms (6½ inches) long, and a larger size varying from about 19 cms (7½ inches) to 21·5 cms (8½ inches). Small specimens in existence are around 7·5–10 cms (3–4 inches).

Wavy-end spoons were a direct descendant of the trefid. They appeared towards the final years of the 17th century and were very similar to the trefid except that the end of the stem was no longer notched. The bowl narrowed and became slightly more pointed, while the rat-tail was often decorated with bead work. By the turn of the century a more elegant line appeared. The stem was far more graceful having by now become waisted and terminating either in a wavy-end or an unbroken semi-circle. It curved gently into the bowl which was still backed by a rat-tail. The end of the stem continued to have a forward curve, thus spoons were placed on the table with the inside of their bowls facing downwards, revealing the decorative back of the bowls.

Within about twenty years of the turn of the century, spoons began to be made in more specific sizes. The large table spoon and the smaller dessert spoon appeared, and with the growing demand for tea, tea spoons began to be made in growing numbers. When tracing development and evolution on these lines it is often difficult to give a specific date for the appearance of a certain type of item or style. Usually it was a gradual development, and one can only say when such objects became more general. American spoons were also evolving from the wavy-end variety, their stems being produced with rounded ends like their English counterparts; these also now having a ridge along the centre, commonly described as the mid-rib.

By the early years of George II's reign the rat-tail began to disappear both in England and America, to be replaced by a small, rounded droplet. With the disappearance of the rat-tail also went the decoration on the back of the bowl for a while, which now became generally plain, the stems becoming rounded at the ends. The ridge along the centre of the stem also gradually disappeared or considerably lessened in length. Now often replacing the simple droplet at the back of the bowl was the fashionable shell motif. By the mid-18th century this had been joined by other shell and scroll decoration cast in low relief, sometimes covering more than half the back of the bowl.

Many and varied forms of decoration now began to embellish the stem. Popular among these was feather edging, an engraved border chased with short oblique lines; the threaded edge, a simple, plain border outline; and the popular beaded edge. Bright-cutting joined them towards the end of the century, in the 1780's, and resulted in an astonishing variety of decoration.

The Onslow pattern, with its wide scrolled turned-down finial, named after Arthur Onslow (1691–1768), Speaker of the House of Commons for thirty-three years, first appeared before 1750, and continued in fashion for many years.

Tea spoons in particular were decorated with various other forms of ornament, including sets with swans, two-headed eagles, flowers, ships and short legends. Other, general designs for all types of spoons included the thread and shell pattern, a plain, narrow border terminating in the popular shell motif at the end of the stem; the king's pattern, ornate also with the shell motif; the heavy queen's pattern; and the husk design. Such decoration, while appearing commonly on the plain, tapering type of spoon, also appeared at a later stage on the fiddle-pattern. This was introduced towards the end of the 18th century and had an entirely different outline for the stem, which was given square-shoulders just above the junction of the bowl. The rounded end of the stem was also squared into an angular shape before it continued down the length towards the bowl. The fiddle pattern proved to be extremely popular and while it might be left plain, it was more usually adorned by one of the designs already mentioned.

One of the most important changes in the basic shape of the spoon occurred during the middle of the 18th century. The spoon began to be made with a stem which balanced the bowl by curving in a direction opposite to it. Thus when the spoon was laid flat on the table, the inside of its bowl facing outwards, the slightly thickened end of the stem now rested on the surface. This design became known as the "Old English" pattern, and has remained more or less the basic outline for spoons ever since that time. Collectors should note, therefore, that a spoon made roughly before the 1760's, however similar it might look to later spoons, can usually be detected by the way the end of the stem curves. If this turns in the same direction as the bowl it is an early spoon; if it curves backwards, the spoon is of a later date.

Important 18th century spoon-makers included Thomas Chawner (spoons were also made prolifically by succeeding members of the Chawner family into the 19th century); Daniel Smith and Robert Sharp; John Crouch and Thomas Hannan; John Wakelin and William Taylor; John Emes; Robert Hennell; and John Schofield. Many other silversmiths also produced spoons, including the Bateman family, and the best way to check their names and dates from the initials which appear on the spoons near the hall-marks is by consulting a copy of *English Goldsmiths and Their Marks* by Sir Charles J. Jackson.

By the end of the rococo period spoons were also being made in America with backward-bending ends; the fronts of the stems being commonly decorated with some form of bright-cutting. The droplet on the back of the bowl was gradually replaced by a popular motif like an acanthus leaf. Sometimes the bowl might be fluted; on others the popular fiddle-pattern was followed. By the turn of the 19th century a new, graceful spoon had appeared in America called the "coffin-end". This meant that the elegant, backward bending stem was squared off, resulting in a pleasing angular effect.

Many tea spoons made during the 18th century are sometimes described as picture-back spoons, a description which relates to the pattern or picture on the back of their bowls. Although they were produced widely by numerous silversmiths, they closely resemble each other. It has been suggested that because of this, some sort of pattern book was available for spoon-makers to copy. As no such pattern books appear to be in existence, it may be just as logical to assume that silversmiths simply copied each other, varying or adapting the patterns to suit themselves. The dove holding an olive branch which was found on American spoons, and which no doubt related to the Olive Branch petition from the American Colonists to George III in 1775 which failed when the King refused to see Richard Penn, was certainly found on English spoons bearing the date of that year. An earlier English spoon-back shows a hen with chicks set in a farmyard scene which sprawls over at least three-quarters of the bowl. Beautiful, but rare, is the little picture of a pyriform teapot which appeared around 1770. Another early example is decorated with a stork which carries a serpent in its beak. Apart from specific pictures, there was also a wide variety of floral designs, all very charming. Sometimes these might be comparatively simple; others perhaps more elaborate. All were vigorous in their ornament and imparted, despite the fact that they were copied extensively, individuality to the spoon which is particular refreshing to the collector to discover, when he turns a spoon over, the prettily decorated bowl.

MOTE SKIMMERS

No chapter which traces the development of the spoon would be complete without devoting space to the mote skimmer. Sometimes called the mote spoon or even stirrer spoon, this simple utensil is quite distinctive in its outline. The bowl is perforated and the rounded, slender stem ends in quite a sharp point. The latter was used to poke clear the perforations at the bottom of the tea-pot spout, while the pierced bowl was used to skim the tea and remove the odd particle of foreign matter (or mote), hence the name, mote skimmer. Mention was made of these dainty utensils as far back as 1697, at which time they were described as long or strainer tea-spoons with narrow painted handles. The word strainer was apt, since they were the original forerunner of the tea strainer, which we use today. Nevertheless, there are differing schools of thought on the purpose of the mote skimmer, although it is commonly agreed that they were used for this primitive form of tea "straining".

In early examples the bowls were given rat-tail strengthening at the junction of the bowl and the stem. The perforations in the bowl were usually small, simple pierced holes. Some mote skimmers were sold occasionally together with other pieces of tea equipage to make a set. Examples from the 18th century have finer piercings, usually in foliated shapes or crosses to form a simple pattern. The rat-tail in these later spoons is replaced by a droplet, shell or some other form of popular motif. American examples, which are rare, were very similar to those made in England, and might be die-struck on the back of the bowl with a flared shell motif; the bowl would be similarly pierced perhaps with crosses forming a central basic pattern, and foliage or scroll piercings around the edges.

Mote skimmers have a charm of their own, and while not among the more important pieces of tea silver, have played an important and functional role in the story of tea equipage. In fact, they must have been quite indispensable when one considers that early tea contained to a certain degree all those unwanted particles which are today removed by mechanical means. There are still many mote skimmers in existence, which is not surprising as they continued to be used for many years, the first tea strainer not appearing on the tea table until well towards the close of the 18th century. Certainly there are more mote skimmers available to collectors than there are early tea strainers which are, in fact, comparatively rare. The writer herself has only seen a handful of these, and one of the earliest was made as late as 1817. This was a delicate little strainer with a hook so that it could be hung when not in use. It was subsequently bought by an American who bore it triumphantly back to his homeland. There are as well very large versions of the mote skimmer. These usually have hall-marks dating from about the 1770's and were used with tea urns.

Tea spoons generally are a rich source from which the collector may derive great satisfaction. Even bearing in mind the fact that their prices have climbed steeply over recent years, they are still among the less expensive items of tea silver and can be collected individually by the beginner. Picture-back spoons, feather-edged, threaded-edged, king's pattern, queen's pattern, fiddle-shape, bright-cut; all are a delight to the eye, and greatly enhance the modern tea table.

Mote skimmers, of course, cannot fulfil a functional purpose in the home today. They are usually collected for their charm and antiquity value. They have always drawn a constant following among collectors, and no doubt will continue to do so, despite the fact that they can no longer be regarded as a less expensive item to collect.

Early spoons, of the knop finial variety, apostle, maidenhead and so on, which are discussed earlier in this chapter, are today sought only by the devoted collector with vast financial resources, although it is still possible for spoons from the in-between period (wavy-e ndand others) to be found for far less sums. And, once acquired, such a spoon may still be used at tea time or special occasions. I have seen a trefid spoon used as a preserve spoon with very great effect, although others may prefer to keep such an acquisition locked in a cabinet. Spoons, in any case, are fascinating to collect and a delight to possess.

CHAPTER FIVE

SUGAR BOWLS AND TONGS

"Love and scandal are the best
sweeteners of tea."

Henry Fielding

The poor relished sweet tea and used large quantities of sugar. By the last decade or so of the 18th century sugar from the British West Indies was to be found on practically every table throughout the land.

During Shakespeare's days, however, only a small amount was imported from Mediterranean ports. Early sugar came into the country in the form of large sugar loaves, which needed to be reduced in size by wielding a chopper. The quantity of sugar imported annually during the reign of Charles II was about 800 tons, and by 1700 England still only consumed the comparatively small amount of 10,000 tons. According to J. C. Drummond, however, in *The Englishman's Food*, by the turn of the 19th century the figure had leapt to 150,000 tons, and as he points out, allowing for the fact that the population had doubled, the average use of sugar by each person had risen seven and a half times during the 18th century.

It is unlikely that silver containers for sugar were made before the 16th century. When they did appear they were used as an appendage to the wine service. By the following century, however, despite the fact that sugar was still hardly a generally consumed commodity, records of silver plate reveal that sugar boxes were not uncommon. One of several references mentions a sugar box spoon as well as a sugar box. Sometimes these very early examples are described as sweetmeat boxes. Such caskets or boxes were usually oval and quite shallow, standing on four feet. They would have a hinged and hasped cover which might have some form of handle

61

in the centre. Others were in the shape of a scallop shell, their lids beautifully embossed. The feet might be in the form of dainty shells or some other complementary shape. Later examples might be engraved all over with *chinoiseries*.

Contemporary American sugar boxes might be adorned with a wide variety of Baroque-style decoration, employing a versatile use of elaborate ornament. One such example by the Boston silver-smith, John Coney, made at the turn of the 18th century is a shallow, oval box upon four scrolled bracket feet of a strange corkscrew shape. The body is divided into twelve rotund lobes with fluting between. They are repeated on the cover in a smaller size and encircle chased acanthus leaves. The handle on this superb piece is shaped like a coiled snake. Another sugar box, also by a Boston silversmith, Edward Winslow, is oval and stands on scroll feet but has impressive decorative work on the body because of the sense of movement which this conveys, being composed of swirls of fluting and gadrooning, punctuated above each leg by acanthus leaves. The cover has more gadrooning together with a positive encrustment of elaborate foliage decoration. The handle is beautiful, based on the acanthus leaf and most elegant.

By the last decade or so of the 17th century, sugar bowls had appeared. J. F. Hayward reveals in *Huguenot Silver in England* that the Earl of Devonshire gave £11.3.3 for a sugar box weighing 32 oz in 1687, paying 7s an ounce for it, which worked out at a trifling amount compared with the £51.16.0 which he spent at that time on a 2-branch candlestick, weighing 172 oz 17 dwt, at 6s an ounce. During this period and back to the Restoration, excessive amounts were spent on silver, embracing domestic items of all kinds. Samuel Pepys was the proud possessor of a silver table.

The new loose-covered sugar bowls, sometimes referred to as sugar dishes, probably derived their hemispherical shape from the Chinese porcelain covered bowls being imported from the East. These comparatively unadorned bowls stood upon a moulded foot-ring, the separate cover resembling a flattish dome, and sur-mounted by an applied moulded ring which served as a handle. It has been suggested, and it is quite likely, that as the cover was deep, it might sometimes have doubled up as a dish for spoons. Other early bowls were octagonal or polygonal in shape. Seldom is there any ornament apart from the most simple or a coat-of-arms.

Towards the third decade of the 18th century, the shape of the English hemispherical bowl began to change, becoming somewhat heavier in outline. Certain forms of decoration also gradually appeared, based on the rococo theme of asymmetry and incorporating other characteristics of the period. American sugar bowls began to resemble more their English counterparts. By the middle of the century English bowls were tending to be ogee-shaped. Later came the version based on a vase form, decorated with swirls of embossing, the cover topped by a finial cast probably in the shape of a pineapple. This design was also popular in America.

After the 1760's, with the dawn of neo-classical styles, new ideas flooded the silversmith's workshop, and the sugar bowl, too, became uniformly elegant. A further vase shape, elongated and more graceful altogether, became popular. Broad at the shoulders, it tapered gently towards a stem which was set on a rounded foot. Two handles either side of the shoulders might be linked with the usual form of Adam-style swags. The high-domed lid might be surmounted by an urn-shaped finial.

Pierced decoration now also became popular. The upper half of the body of the vessel might be pierced with geometric patterns and enriched with embossing. The lower half might be embossed and chased in such a way as to echo this design and also to accentuate the natural grace of the vase shape. The cover decoration would match or complement the lower half, while the stem would be pierced to match the upper piercing. A deep blue glass liner would reveal the delicacy of the pierced work. From about the last quarter of the 18th century this shape was also popular unpierced. A wider shaped bowl, elliptical in outline, with a pair of slender recurved handles, starting at the rim and recurving down to the base, became extremely popular.

The vase or urn shaped bowl was produced in America to a very high standard by leading silversmiths. Generally known as sugar urns, they are among the best examples produced during the neo-classical period. The proportions were excellent, and the decoration which was often bright-cut was of first-class workmanship.

After about the first half of the 18th century, the lids of sugar bowls had gradually disappeared, and this in its turn brought about the development of an arching type of handle to be placed on the modest little vessel known as the sugar bucket. It, too, might be pierced, and contain the familiar blue glass liner, or it might be decorated in another, more simple fashion. Sometimes it might have a high-spreading foot, but more often it lacked this, presenting a simple, unassuming shape, perfectly acceptable in itself. It is thought that these bucket-shaped bowls might also have been used for cream or even jam, but as they are known to have been included in tea chests with a pair of canisters, replacing the sugar bowl, it has naturally been assumed that they were intended for sugar.

From about 1780, silversmiths generally were prolific in their output of the elliptical, boat-shaped sugar basket with a central swinging handle. These would either be solid and garnished with neo-classical decoration, or they would be pierced and incorporate the blue glass liner. Small wonder that they were so popular, since they stood gracefully upon a short stem which spread out into a rounded foot, and presented a most attractive addition to the tea silver. Large numbers were produced by the new factory methods, and as a result many still remain today.

American designs in this shape closely resembled the English, and a beautiful, well-known example by Paul Revere typifies this. Exquisitely fluted, it stands on an elegant stem which is set off by a curvaceous round foot. It has a central swing handle. A later example by Josiah H. Lownes, owned by the Henry Ford Museum, Dearborn, Michigan, has two slender recurving handles which trace the outline of the side of the bowl. It is simply but effectively decorated with a small amount of engraving.

Until roughly the mid-18th century, sugar baskets were usually made as individual pieces, complementing the rest of the tea equipage. From about this time, however, a new fashion dictated that a trio of two canisters and one sugar box should be kept together in a tea chest. Both the canisters and the box closely resembled each other, the latter being replaced in some later chests by the sugar pail, already described, and by a lidded flint-glass bowl.

By the end of the 18th century, sugar bowls of an oval shape with a flat bottom were made as part of the numerous tea services which were then being produced in growing numbers. They were

6. Tea urn with ball-shaped body, popular from the last decade of the 18th century. (C. Shapland and Company)

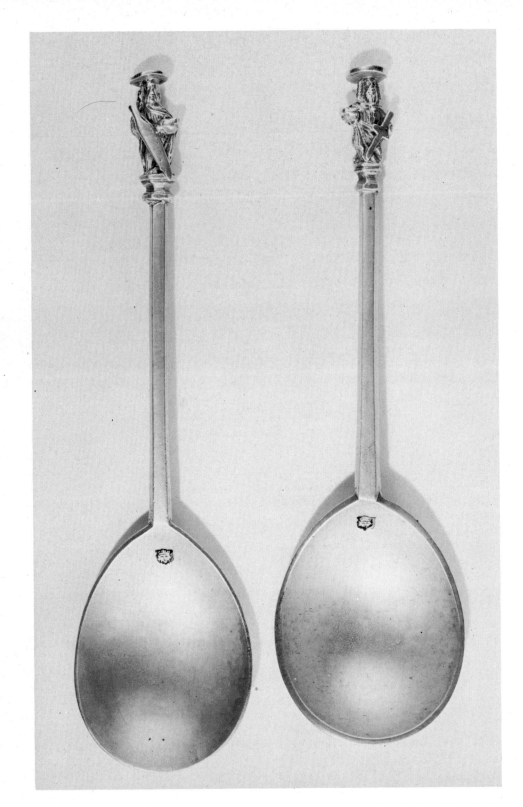

17. Two 17th century apostle spoons, left, St. Bartholomew, carrying a butcher's knife, maker's mark, R.C., c. 1633; right, St. Philip, carrying a pastoral staff, makers mark D enclosing a C, c. 1636. (Garrard and Company Ltd.)

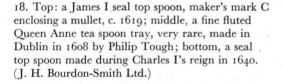

18. Top: a James I seal top spoon, maker's mark C
enclosing a mullet, c. 1619; middle, a fine fluted
Queen Anne tea spoon tray, very rare, made in
Dublin in 1608 by Philip Tough; bottom, a seal
top spoon made during Charles I's reign in 1640.
(J. H. Bourdon-Smith Ltd.)

19. An Elizabethan apostle spoon, London 1599,
showing the maker's mark at the back of the stem
near the bowl. (Phillips)

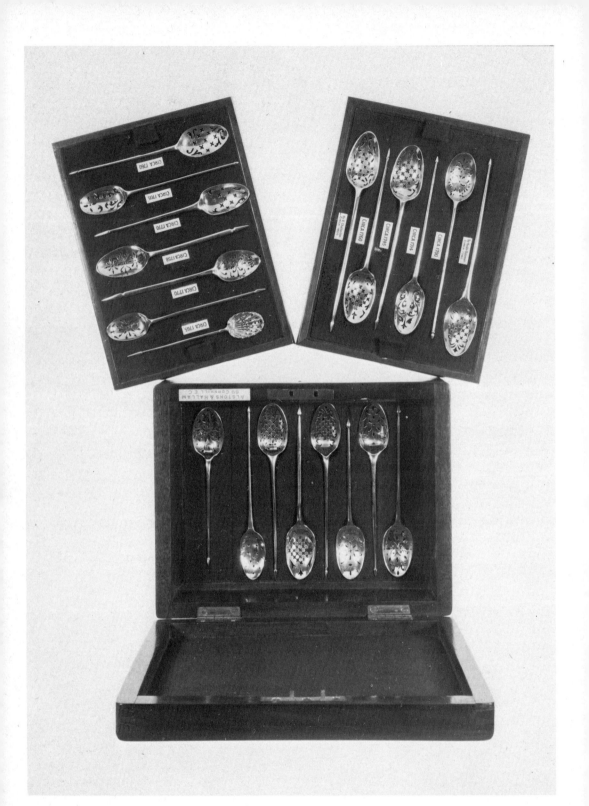

20. A collection of 18th century mote skimmers. (S. J. Shrubsole Ltd.)

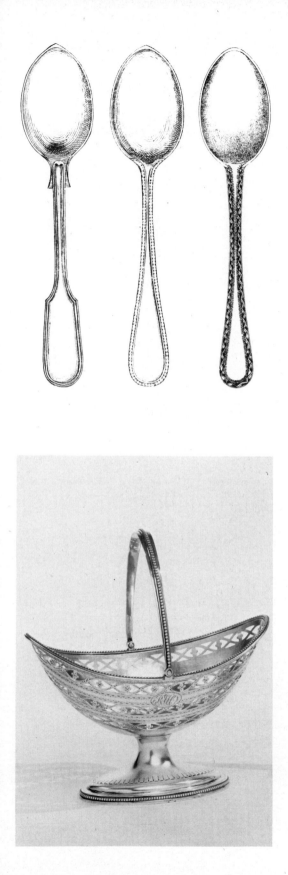

21. Three tea spoons, left to right: fiddle thread pattern; beaded stem; bright-cut stem.

22. Late 18th century pierced sugar basket with hinged handle and short, elegant stem. The rim of the basket is strengthened by beading, which also decorates the foot and handle. (S. J. Shrubsole Ltd.)

23. An American sugar urn and cover, unmarked, c. 1790. (Spink and Son Ltd.)

24. Scissor-type sugar tongs, enriched with cast naturalistic motifs. (Phillips)

25. Left to right: helmet-type milk jug by George Hodder with Cork hall-mark, 1760–70; embossed pear-shaped jug set on three hoof feet by William Hughes, Dublin, 1760–70; a contemporary London jug, maker's mark, H.C., c. 1765. embossed helmet-shaped jug, c. 1760. (Victoria and Albert Museum)

26. Cow-shaped milk jug, London, c. 1766.

27. Top, left to right: Made during the reign of George III, in 1802; marked with the initials DM, and made in 1763; made during the reign of George IV in 1825, makers mark, W.E. Bottom, left to right: beautifully bright-cut, this octagonal jug is by A. Peterson, 1797; sparsely decorated and made in 1788; typical neo-classical decoration by R. Hennell, 1792. (J. H. Bourdon-Smith Ltd.)

28. A milk jug by P. and A. Bateman, 1791, and a George III sugar basket, maker John Robins, 1782. (Phillips)

29. An American three-piece tea set of vase shape, embossed with flowers and fruit on a matted background, the finial a strawberry and the handles decorated to complement the decoration on the bodies. Made by A. E. Warner, c. 1820. (Phillips)

later shaped variously, and some were placed on four ball feet, while others had narrow foot-rings. When fashion returned to the over-indulged revived rococo, sugar bowls in common with the rest of the tea silver became elaborately embossed. The thirst for this form of decoration seemed as unquenchable as the thirst for tea. Thus the sugar bowl, although its direct descendant, bore no resemblance at all to the exquisite little shell-shaped sugar box in use when James I was on the throne. Only the contents proved that the two were related.

SUGAR TONGS

Today the small sugar spoon or dainty tongs rest inside the sugar bowl for the sole purpose of conveying the sugar from bowl to cup. Early utensils designed to aid this function also needed to be able to crack sugar from the loaf. Steel sugar nippers did this to perfection. Early 18th century sugar tongs looked rather like scissors with looped handles, for ease of gripping. At the end of their attractive scrolled stems were claws to hold the sugar which might also be shaped like shells. A later design of the scissor-shaped tong resembled the outline of a stork, the legs terminating in a circular pattern to form grips for the fingers, while the long beak opened to grasp the sugar. The scissor-shape continued in use for many decades, until roughly the middle of the 18th century. Gradually it was replaced in popularity by the more familiar bow-shaped tongs.

Although bow-shaped tongs began to appear generally around this time, far earlier examples had, in fact, been in use. They were made in five pieces: a rounded piece of silver connecting the arms, made springy by hammering; a pair of arms; and two holders for the sugar, commonly shaped like claws or shells. These pieces were simply soldered together.

Tongs were decorated in a variety of ways. They might be chased, engraved, pierced or bright-cut. And when the fiddle-pattern became popular (described in the chapter on spoons), they appeared in this style, too. After about the last decade of the 18th century, pierced sugar tongs tended to disappear. Bright-cutting superseded this form of decoration in popularity, and some very fine examples of this form of engraving were produced. Thus, until the first few years of the 19th century, sugar tongs were slender and delicate, beautifully engraved and usually nicely executed. During this time, tongs possessed flat, tapering stems and were in demand as additional matching items to sets of tea spoons. After the turn of the century, however, they became quite plain, the fashion for bright-cutting diminished and they were far less attractive. Even the grips lacked interest and became as plain as the rest of the tongs, which seldom now possessed more than a threaded edge for decoration. By the second decade, sugar tongs had generally increased in thickness of metal and length, and were thus in proportion to the large ceramic sugar bowls commonly used in most homes. Those which were made to match other pieces of tea silver generally retained a more dainty form.

Sugar tongs are among the less expensive items of tea silver, and they are still as useful today as they have always been. Many of them were made in Birmingham, and therefore bear the Birmingham anchor. They sometimes lack a complete set of hall-marks or perhaps one or two of the marks might be missing. The earlier, delicate tongs often broke, and in the repairing of them the hall-marks might also have become obscured.

Apart from buying sugar tongs as useful and decorative pieces of silver for the home, it is also interesting to build up a collection, including the very early scissor-shape, the decorated later 18th century variety, the bright-cut examples and one or two of the 19th century heavier examples. Fiddle-shaped tongs can be matched to fiddle-shaped spoons; bright-cut specimens likewise to similarly cut bright-cut tea spoons. The variety is endless and prices not so prohibitive as to inhibit one's enthusiasm, as many types are certainly still cheap enough for the beginner and beautiful enough for the true lover of old silver.

CHAPTER SIX

MILK JUGS, CREAM JUGS AND
TEA SERVICES

*"Look here, steward, if this is coffee I want
tea; but if this is tea than I wish for coffee."*

Punch, *1902*

Silver jugs have remained in constant demand throughout the centuries. Their uses are numerous, yet it is unlikely that milk jugs were made before the early years of the 18th century.

Some examples produced during the first few years of the 18th century were not unlike small versions of the beer jug, being rotund and functional with two simple lines of moulding running around the body at its widest girth. They are balanced nicely by quite a wide splayed foot ring. Others, less rounded, stand on a narrow, moulded ring. The scroll handles and open spouts may be at right angles to each other. Many early examples are quite diminutive, being no more than about 7·5 cms (3 inches) high. Apart from those with lines of moulding, most are completely lacking in decoration, or perhaps may bear an engraved coat-of-arms.

In the oil painting by Richard Collins, depicting the Gay family at tea, which is reproduced in this book, there is a tall, lidded jug. It is virtually impossible to know whether this was intended for hot water or hot milk. By its size it seems more likely that it was used for the former, yet in this case it seems strange that a milk jug should be missing from such a complete set of tea equipage. As some people probably still preferred their tea clear, the jug could presumably have been used for either.

However, as the early Georgians had already developed a strong taste for tea, no doubt somewhere along the line many must have decided that they preferred the aromatic flavour tempered with a little milk. Thus the small jug now became more common, hammered up from the flat, with the spout and handle placed opposite each other. The early examples had been made from sections of cast silver. The foot ring still remained cast, as were the spout and handle, although towards the third decade of the century, the spout began to be fashioned out of the body. Moulded ornamentation continued to be the main type of decoration, appearing on the foot, sometimes on the rim of the body and also beneath the spout. This type of jug remained popular well into the second half of the 18th century, and such examples still remain available for the enthusiastic collector.

Early American jugs were very similar, although there are few of them. They were usually pear-shaped and stood on a splayed foot, similar to contemporary sugar bowls. They occasionally had hinged covers, and were mostly made by John Edwards and Jacob Hurd of Boston.

By the third decade of the century a new form evolved in England. The helmet-shaped water ewer no doubt served as the inspiration for this. Silversmiths now took this shape and scaled it down to the proportions of a small jug. The result was surprisingly successful. Rather like an inverted helmet, this elegant jug was hammered up from one sheet of silver, the broad spout being an integral part of the body. Its graceful, fluid lines thus rose un-interrupted from base to rim. It was set on a spreading moulded foot. Although the spout was part of the body, the handle was still cast and soldered on. Ewer-shaped jugs were also set upon three cast feet, and towards the middle of the century this fashion spread to the popular pear-shaped jugs, which now appeared on three cast hoof or scroll feet.

Until roughly this time jugs were comparatively plain and were usually devoid of much ornamentation. Gilding was occasionally used but was not all that general as it naturally added to the cost. When the rococo period of decoration began, some jugs naturally came under its influence. These would be chased or embossed with scrolls, shells, flowers and even certain types of scenes, those con-cerned with hunting being particularly popular. Some became quite elaborately decorated, with a mass of rococo inspired orna-mentation embellishing much of the surface; in others it might cover the whole vessel.

An American jug of this period by Jacob Hurd closely resembles its English pear-shaped counterpart, with a dainty, curvey rim broadening into the everted spout. It is set upon three cabriole legs, and has the customary type of scene to be found on English jugs, showing pastoral scenes and a view of Fort William Castle. There is very little about either its shape or decoration, except, of course, the subject matter, which would differentiate it in any way from a contemporary English jug at a first cursory glance.

The handles of milk jugs justify special mention because these can be a useful guide when dating a piece. The simple C and S scrolls which appeared on early jugs were later succeeded by more sophisticated versions. Sometimes these might be decorated by gadrooning, reeding or beading. Often a chased acanthus leaf would appear on the top of the handle, or this might be quite plain and flat, forming a thumb rest. A number of decorative handles based on the scroll were thus in use throughout the 18th century. Some, when examined in profile, recurved to such an extent that they seemed almost to meander in outline before finally terminating in something like a volute tail. At the top they would be embellished by a moulded and chased motif or some other ornament like the mask of the ram, in full relief. Handles of American jugs are based on the same intricate flowing and recurving scroll outlines.

Likewise, jug legs made by silversmiths from both countries are very similar. They echo the shapes and designs of the legs which appeared on current furniture of the period, and might terminate in ball-and-claw, hoofs, paws, or the pad. The legs which were of the graceful cabriole shape, like their wooden counterparts, would have pronounced decorated knees bearing cyclic motifs. Where the legs joined the body of the jug, the junction would be concealed by further decoration. An American jug by Samuel Casey of Rhode Island is a perfect example. The graceful handle is of double-scroll form, while the feet are of the ball-and-claw type found on contemporary furniture. The rim is a dainty escalloped shape, and the body has an asymmetrical chased pattern. Another by Philip Hulbeart in the Philadelphia Museum of Art is heavily decorated with naturalistic chasing, and the complicated scroll handle is quite distinctive of the period. The legs which terminate in a shell have additional decorative adornments in the form of ornate masks.

The florid rococo style remained buoyant until the opposing ideas of the neo-classical era eclipsed it. The new period brought with it a wealth of classical design undreamt of before. Rococo work was ousted almost immediately from its reigning platform of fashion and was forgotten until its revival in the following century.

A jug more suited to contain cream than milk now came on to the scene. This was an elegant boat shape, and while it had the same form as the helmet jug, its body was lower and wider.

The barrel shaped jug which was copied greatly in ceramics made its appearance in the sixties. It had only a slight neck and the lip was quite small. It stood on a moulded foot. During this period the dropped bottom set on a high moulded circular foot appeared on many milk jugs.

An unusual style, and one which usually seems to appeal to collectors, is the milk jug in the shape of the cow. These became popular roughly during the last three decades of the 18th century. The cow was made in pieces and soldered together. The beast's curled tail was appropriately placed so as to serve as a handle, while the jug was filled through a hole in the top of the back, which was covered by a hinged lid, not unlike a saddle. This might be plain or decorated with an engraved naturalistic design. Sometimes the knob used to lift the lid might be in the form of a fly. The milk was actually poured through the cow's mouth. Some form of decoration representing hair might appear on the head and body; on others this was omitted. The cow jug was made in many cases by a London craftsman, John Schuppe (who worked as a silversmith for twenty years from 1753 to 1773). He probably emigrated from the Netherlands where jugs of this type had been produced earlier. There are, however, other cow jugs which bear the marks of various silversmiths.

The new rolling processes now being used by manufacturing silversmiths meant that the silver plate became so thinly rolled that many neo-classical jugs were extremely frail. In fact, the rolling-mill had been in use for about fifty years already, but during the 1760's and onwards developments in machinery meant that machines could duplicate as many times as required the operations of stamping, embossing or piercing. Whereas at one time this work had involved several craftsmen, all that was now needed was a stamping machine. Such a machine, which was patented in London in the late 1760's, and very quickly improved upon, meant that individual sections could be shaped and patterns pierced quickly and efficiently. Improved rolling-mills resulted in flimsy silver which was quickly made into cheaper articles needing some form of additional strengthening. The rims of jugs, for instance, were often strengthened with tiny punched beads. Candlesticks required some form of interior strengthening, and they also needed to have their feet weighted for stability.

From the silver factories using the new methods there now poured a flow of smaller domestic items including jugs, spoons, tea pots, sugar bowls, caddies, casters, cake baskets and trays. They came from the new manufacturing areas of Sheffield and Birmingham, challenging the position of the London silversmiths who had always reigned supreme. Although the new methods meant that fine items of silver could now be enjoyed by others with less wealth, those who could afford it, or wanted something distinguished, inevitably still commissioned an object to be hand-made. These pieces stand out distinctly from the mass-produced miscellanea of the late 18th century and onwards.

With this flood of silver based on neo-classical shapes and styles came new outlines for the cream jug. The body, sometimes octagonal, tapered gracefully to the base, an elegant stem meeting it from the circular or oval concave foot, not uncommonly mounted on a four-sided plinth. More elegance appeared with the handle, which now rose from the rim and swept down to the base in a graceful recurving outline. Such jugs were usually made in two pieces and soldered together. The foot was also an entirely separate piece. Decoration, which was typical of the period and which was used on other forms of silver, included body engraving and bright-cutting.

American cream jugs also followed these refined lines, standing on a slender stem, with a graceful handle, sometimes recurving, sweeping towards the body and emphasising the general shape. When such jugs were made as part of a tea set, they usually echoed precisely the line and form of the tea pot and sugar urn, but were almost more graceful because of their smaller size necessitating more slender proportions.

Until the last years of the 18th century the silver cream jug was generally made separately. It was not part of a tea service or tea set. However, because the cheaper factory methods of Sheffield and Birmingham had resulted in an unprecedented demand for domestic silver, there arose a natural market for tea services, consisting of a tea pot, sugar basin and cream jug. The thinly rolled silver now in use made it possible to meet this demand at competitive prices, and the idea of a tea service of this type, once born, remained for ever. Later sets also included a coffee pot. It has been suggested that the names cream ewer and cream jug can be traced back to the days when these early factories first produced thin, inexpensive milk jugs so prolifically.

Another form of cream jug which became fashionable towards the end of the 18th century was deprived of a stem foot and given a wide, oval body on a flat base. It had a loop handle which rose vertically from the rim and narrow, everted spout. The rim was commonly strengthened with moulding of the reeded variety, and the lower part of the body was often decorated with some popular and current form of ornament. An interesting American example by Paul Revere (Museum of Fine Arts, Boston) brings a remarkable delicacy to this undelicate shape. It is beautifully engraved with a dainty classical pattern around the high waist, and the base is further enhanced with a vertical pattern which gives an elongated effect to the jug. The rim is strengthened by reeding, and the sweeping handle is reeded to match.

By the first decade of the 19th century, in common with some tea pots, the jug was raised upon four ball-shaped feet. When George IV came to the throne this type of jug had evolved into a squatter shape. The ball-shaped feet had become transformed into shapely scrolls, usually moulded in one piece with the base rim, and lavish embossing covered the sides. The handle was similarly embellished with naturalistic decoration as was the rim with its strengthening applied moulding. By the third decade of the century the melon-shaped jug had become popular. Succeeding years saw revivals of various 18th century styles and these are dealt with fully in the chapter on Victorian tea silver.

TEA SERVICES
By the turn of the 19th century, the silver tea service was becoming quite a common purchase. All those who could possibly aspire to such heights sought eagerly to avail themselves of this prestigious

form of domestic plate. Tea services now began to appear in large numbers. The elegant classical lines of the Adam period mingled with, and were gradually superseded by, the rounded melon shape, heavily decorated with a fantasy of rococo embossing, being used for cream and milk jugs. An astonishing variety of styles and decorative effects emerged from Birmingham and Sheffield. Among these were tea services incorporating the fashionable peaked-top tea pot, either on a foot or ball-shaped feet. Handles would either be of silver, with suitable inlets of insulating material, or of bone.

American silversmiths were just as prolific during this period. While much of their tea silver continued to be in neo-classical lines, the workmanship generally of a high calibre, by the first decade of the 19th century American tea services, too, began to emerge from this influence. An interesting Philadelphian service consists of pieces made by three individual silversmiths. The slop bowl, tea and coffee pot are by Samuel Williamson (working 1794–1813), both having concave shoulder form and carved scroll wooden handles with up-curled leaf grips; the cream jug and sugar urn are by Daniel Dupuy, Jr. (1717–1807), the latter also having concave shoulders, but not so pronounced; while the tongs of the spring "U" type, or bow-shape, are by Joseph Richardson, Jr. An unusual characteristic of the slop bowl and sugar urn is the delicately pierced vertical rim, which surmounts a beaded edge.

In the 19th century shapes became bolder and squatter. Ball-shaped feet appeared in America around the turn of the century as they did in England. A service made during the first few years of the 19th century by New York silversmith, William Thompson, combines both ball-shaped feet with ball-and-claw, the latter appearing on the sugar box and the cream jug. The ball feet support the circular foot ring of the slop bowl and the oblong tea pot. Numerous styles and decorations now appeared, and the Empire tea service by William Seal, owned by the Henry Ford Museum, although based on the same broad, rotund shape evolves to a much grander form of decoration. Owls with outstretched wings replace the modest ball-shaped feet. Ornament abounds on this fine Empire example. Bands of machine-rolled basket-weave decoration embellish all four pieces in this service, which are set on short circular stems mounted on four-sided plinths. The magnificent spout of the tea pot culminates in a swan's head and tapers into the body with a grand, chased floral design; rams' heads surmount the rims of the sugar bowl and slop bowl; and large finials shaped like swans surmount the domed covers of the tea pot and sugar bowl.

Hot on the heels of the Empire style in America came the revived rococo which subsequently enjoyed just as much renewed popularity there as it did in England. By the mid-19th century its popularity was toppled by other revivals including the overwhelming Renaissance fashion which lasted until around 1880.

CHAPTER SEVEN

CAKE BASKETS, SUGAR CASTERS, MUFFINEERS AND TRAYS

". . . tea does our fancy aid,
Repress those vapours which the head invade,
And keeps that palace of the soul serene."
                    Edmund Waller

Table baskets are among the most feminine pieces of silver. They are invariably beautiful, generally highly decorative and often exquisitely made. Even some of the later examples, produced by factory methods, still have much to commend them by modern standards. Because of their elegance of shape, most will fit into any kind of home and they are always useful. When not being utilised they can be relied upon to bring an element of gracious living into the room, whether their beauty shines forth from side-board, table or display cabinet.

During the late 16th and early 17th centuries, new foods and ways of serving them necessitated the production of new forms of domestic plate suitable for the dining table and not the buffet. The circular silver table basket was among the first of these early pieces designed for the table, and happily this ornamental piece has remained with us ever since.

Very early baskets, which are extremely rare, are of heavy silver and quite dissimilar to the delicate version made during the 18th century. The latter reflects the gracious tea ritual of the elegant house where the proffering of tea-time delicacies from such baskets well fitted the studied manners of the period.

Early examples would be chased with fruit and foliage patterns, together with other current forms of decoration including arab-esque scrolls, cherubs' heads and eagles' heads. Piercing such work meant that the background needed to be laboriously cut away to remove the metal in order that these ornamental motifs might be revealed in all their splendour. Early craftsmen, assiduous and artistic, carried the overall decorative effect through to the rim which was carefully shaped to complement the main work. A simple, moulded foot-rim was necessary for additional stability. Towards the middle of the 17th century this foot-rim had become more ornate, with a concave spread which might be vertically pierced, the junction of the foot-rim and basket being concealed with cable wire. Because the piercing methods were so crude, much trimming and polishing was necessary to complete the work satisfactorily. Gradually the rims became more widely everted, and piercing and embossing more sophisticated, with flower, leaf or animal motifs. Generally speaking, these designs in piercing and embossing continued until about the first three decades of the 18th century.

Immigrant Huguenot silversmiths have received much praise down the centuries for their finely pierced and embossed baskets. Yet, although their skill cannot be denied, their achievement was also made possible by the English invention of the rolling-mill, which first made its appearance in the last decade of the 17th century and which had been improved greatly by 1728. The fine-gauge sheets of silver of uniform thickness which the mill produced meant that more delicate and complicated patterns could now be used.

The Huguenots who, after various problems, were gradually gaining the recognition they deserved in England, knew fully, with their expertise, how to exploit the potential of the finer silver. Although they have become famous for their superlative work, they were not alone in their achievements. Georgian silversmiths generally began to produce a most wonderful and varied selection of pierced cake and fruit baskets, rectangular, oval and circular, most of which bear evidence of their combined skill and creativity. It was not long before these beautiful pieces of work had become most lucrative and important to the silversmith.

One of the more usual patterns was a series of finely pierced diamonds and circles. The rim would incorporate appliqué decoration, possibly edged with beading, and the inserted, flat base would include further chased patterns of ornate design, sometimes surrounding the coat-of-arms. The handles, of horizontal D-loop

76

shape, were attached beneath the rim. During the 1730's, these two handles were gradually replaced by a single swing handle and, in fact, the oval-shaped basket with its swing handle continued to be produced in comparatively prolific quantities until the final years of the 18th century. By about the fourth decade, the complete basket was commonly raised from a single sheet of silver.

Among Huguenot silversmiths, the name of Paul de Lamerie (1688–1751) has become particularly associated with pierced table baskets. The workmanship of these is superb and the piercing intricate. Some look like amazingly fine and elaborate wicker-work baskets; others are composed of swirling rococo forms, pierced in a complex pattern around both the main body of the basket and the rim. There are those elegantly shaped as deep scallop shells, fluted and pierced with complementing scallop-shaped rims, standing on graceful dolphin feet. Many of these fine baskets were copied by lesser silversmiths who modified the complexity of the work to suit their own techniques and their customers' pockets.

Everted rims generally echoed in full the theme of the main pattern, growing ever more expansive and elaborate. The foot-rim might be replaced by short, graceful legs in cast silver shaped in some current form generally fashionable. Volute and ball-and-claw feet were quite common. Pains were taken to see that the body junction was concealed beneath a suitable form of decoration. As the rococo influence gained strength, patterns became correspondingly more vigorous. Feet, masks and aprons were shortly cast in a single rim, the motifs in high relief corresponding to those on the rim. This highly decorative ring would contain the base of the basket.

By the fourth decade of the 18th century, the great progress which had been made in the design of tea silver included the cake or table basket. Rims were now shaped in such a way as to allow as much of the interior as possible to be seen at a glance. The elaborate and beautiful work of the piercing was thus revealed. The outer borders and rims continued the main theme of this intricate work, being themselves sometimes gracefully curved or scalloped, and incorporating upon the more opulent pieces not only chased and cast appliqué work, but masks of animal faces or other decorative effects veering towards ostentation.

The finely pierced patterns consisted of intricate arrangements of scrolls, circles, crescents and an assortment of other suitable shapes, varying in sizes and gradings. A later favoured pattern consisted of solid panels juxtapositioned with alternate arrangements of crosses and scroll piercings. Handles, too, were carefully decorated to complement or match the overall effect. Some of these became exceedingly pretty in their own right. Some might be twisted to form a cable design; others might be only beaded; there were those which consisted of entwining silver wires; while further examples very much resembled the handles used on kettles of the period.

After about the middle of the 18th century, pierced patterns on the rim practically superseded appliqué work, although it must always be remembered that provincial silversmiths continued with familiar methods and styles usually long after they had been abandoned by the fashionable craftsmen in London. Well into the second half of the century, for example, the old piercing method of embossing the design and cutting away the background might still be used by provincial silversmiths. But craftsmen generally were always behind those pandering to the whims of fashion in London. Furniture design in particular progressed quite slowly in the country areas, where old-established styles continued to be produced long after they had become outmoded in London. This is a contributary reason for the difficulty in saying exactly when a style ceased.

London silversmiths by this time had progressed to a very elaborate form of piercing achieved by the new fly-presses, which could punch small work with extreme accuracy. These fashionable oval-shaped baskets would be composed of various panels, each with its own intricate pierced pattern, perhaps of circles, diamonds, scrolls or quatrefoils, all punched by the new fly-press. Several of the panels would be needed to make the sides of a single basket. They would then be soldered together to form the required oval shape, this soldering being virtually concealed by a decorative beading.

This mass-production of pierced work ultimately led to what can be described as the first of its kind in factory production. The silversmith would purchase the required type and number of pierced panels, then join these in his own workshop. Embellishing and decorating the finished article himself, he would achieve a considerably individual end result. Great versatility, as well as much repetition, were the two opposed consequences of the new methods. In some cases, each single panel used in a basket might differ not only in shape but also in pattern. As there might be as many as thirty patterns available, the diversity and range was considerable. The panels in more ambitious baskets would be artistically married with rococo castings and presswork, and the overall effect was positively sumptuous.

Another type of table basket was made of silver wire, and appeared after the first half of the century. The framework consisted entirely of wire, enveloped with ornamental hammered and chased motifs including sprays of wheat, flowers and vine leaves. Naturalistic arrangements composed of such pastoral delights were extremely popular, although early examples are scarce because they were so delicate that they tended to break easily. The silver wire basket continued in fashion well into the first quarter of the 19th century.

During the last two decades or so of the 18th century, two-handled baskets again became fashionable. The sides of these were pierced in such a way as to give an openwork lattice effect. The rims were embossed with flowers and blossoms or other naturalistic forms, and the whole effect was very charming. These baskets were not so deep as those with swing handles, and stood upon narrow, pierced foot-rims. Another style produced a little later, also with two handles, was pierced in such a way as to look like openwork flat rings and overlapping loops, the end of which formed a trellis. The bases of these were usually set upon plain foot-rims. A heavier style produced during this period was raised from a single piece of silver and embossed on the rim with classical motifs. Any piercings would also be based on such motifs.

In America, Myer Myers produced an elegant basket among the small number which were made during the 1760's. It can be seen at the Metropolitan Museum of Art, New York, and follows closely the current English style. Panels of complex pierced work alternate with each other. The foot-rim of this shallow, oval basket is similarly pierced to complement the rest of the decoration. The handle is of a simple latticed, criss-cross pattern.

More unusual in design and decoration is a later American basket by Simeon Bayley, made towards the end of the century.

79

Its boat-shape is set upon a high splayed foot, and except for the double line of naturalistic pattern on the rim which is echoed in the foot-rim, and an ornate cartouche with initials, the surface is left plain. This emphasises not only the shape of the basket, but the unusual rim which has been formed to give an angular effect. The handle, composed of a double half-circle pierced pattern, is also angular in outline to complement the rim. This shallow basket is a highly individual piece and is beautifully executed throughout.

By around the last decade of the 18th century, the silver table basket was in a general state of decline. Mass-production methods had taken their toll of the fine craftsmanship apparent in earlier work. Further progress in machines meant that Matthew Boulton's steam-operated rolling-mills were enabling the production of a very thin silver, and this, together with factory piercing and the fact that the finished baskets were receiving less hand-decorating or additional ornament, resulted in a rather nondescript object of uniform similarity, made of flimsy silver.

CASTERS AND MUFFINEERS

Although casters may not fall strictly into the description of tea equipage, they greatly warrant a mention in this connection since they often appear at tea time, perhaps to sprinkle sugar over strawberries or small tartlets. Added to this is the fact that many people are interested in these attractive pieces, and all lovers of old silver attempt to acquire one at some time or other.

Many early casters were made in sets of three, the large one being for sugar, and the two smaller ones for black and cayenne pepper. Single pepper casters were also much in evidence, however, and as they usually had large perforations, probably because the pepper was coarsely ground, they can also be used as sugar casters today. Sometimes the caster intended for cayenne pepper might be used for mustard, and in this case the top was left unpierced, but given instead a suitably engraved pattern. On others there might be an inner lining which closed the perforations.

Although some early 18th century casters are straight-sided, either cylindrical or octagonal, occasionally with a simple scroll handle, more usual are the baluster or pyriform shapes. The pyriform, or pear-shaped caster, replaced with formal elegance the more basic charm of the early straight-sided specimens. It was supported by a moulded foot, and surmounting its gently curving outline was a pierced domed cover, neatly topped by a cast finial in the form of an acorn, baluster or acanthus leaf. Usually these beautiful casters were left undecorated, perhaps having a single horizontal band of moulding around the widest perimeter of the pear-shape. The covers were removed by simply pulling them off, and their piercings, like those of cylindrical casters, were usually vertical patterns of scrolls and crosses. This form of caster was made for many years, until at least the first half of the 18th century.

The baluster caster, which was the other popular shape, differed from the pyriform outline by being broader in circumference just below the cover. Thus, with the cover on it seems to swell out almost in the centre. It is thought that this shape might have been inspired by the porcelain baluster vases then being imported from China.

By about 1715, the pyriform caster was also being made octagonal in form, which considerably enhanced the overall effect. Although casters were generally left undecorated, at the time when rococo influence was at its greatest, this form of caster might be generously embossed and given an ornate cartouche. The plainer examples were still given added horizontal mouldings or gadrooning. From about the fourth decade, the ogee shape became popular.

An exquisite little cylindrical caster by Gerrit Onckelbag, made during the first few years of the 18th century and in a private American collection, is one of the best New York examples of this period. The cover is unusual, being almost flat-topped, while the splayed-out foot is gadrooned and fluted. Above the reeded base is a formal leaf pattern. The piercings are scanty, and the engraving on the cover sparse, and this contrasts well with the decorative effects below. Similar casters were made by Boston silversmiths.

Another beautiful American caster by Bartholomew Le Roux, also made during this period, is very similar to one produced by Richard Biggs of London about 1701. Both have gadrooned foot-rims and horizontal moulding applied, but while the Le Roux example has crudely pierced holes, that by Biggs is quite finely pierced in a fairly intricate pattern. The engraving on both of these cylindrical casters is of the simple naturalistic style.

The reign of George III saw a revival in the fashion for cylindrical casters with high dome covers, popular at the turn of the 18th century. An important difference with the later casters, of course, was that their covers were delicately pierced with neoclassical motifs. It was not unusual at this time to find sets of six small casters, or those with pierced sides which were fitted with blue glass liners, similar to the pierced sugar bowls of the period.

The vase shape now so popular with all pieces of tea silver was also apparent in the design of casters, which were made in large numbers by silversmiths in London, Birmingham and Sheffield, from about the last decade of the 18th century, well into the first quarter of the 19th century. Copies of earlier shapes and styles were also made during this period.

Sometimes the word "dredger" is used for the casters which have a handle attached. These were made from the early years of the 18th century, usually with simple scroll handles and little decoration, except perhaps horizontal moulding. Although these may have been intended for kitchen use, it seems unlikely as silver was always expensive. More plausible is the theory that they were intended for the sprinkling of spices, such as cinnamon, since this was an indulgence much beloved during the 18th century.

Very early dredgers, made towards the final years of the 17th century, usually stood about 10 cms (4 inches) high. They were extremely simple, cylindrical in shape with a spreading foot-rim. A sparse amount of gadrooning or moulding might relieve the overall plainness. The cover was usually low-domed, with crude circular perforations. The body, it can be detected, was not worked up from the flat in a single piece, but formed from the metal rolled flat and soldered together in a vertical seam; the circular base being made separately, inserted then soldered.

While earlier dredgers were octagonal, there was a return to the plain, cylindrical shape after about the 1730's, sometimes decorated in the rococo style. By the end of the 18th century, when people took a delight in sprinkling cinnamon on hot buttered muffins, a small, dainty caster took over the job of the simple dredger. Minus the handle, it became known as a muffineer. These were charming little objects, usually vase-shaped, commonly about 10 cms (4 inches) in height. They had low-domed covers with fine circular holes. Examples of the 18th century were quite often decorated with embossing or engraving, but later muffineers were usually plain. A further type was fret-cut in a formal pattern and contained a blue glass liner. A band of moulding was added around the middle to strengthen these.

TRAYS

The origins of the tray can probably be traced back as far as the 15th century when wine or ale in the dining halls of the great was pre-tasted by a servant to ensure that it was free from poison. The goblet would then be replaced on a metal plate. This decisive procedure was prosaically known as the "try". Later, the cover of the drinking-cup came to be used for this purpose, and it is thought that the cover probably acquired the name of the "try" because of the part it played.

Trays have been known under various names ever since, including tazza, salver and waiter. Although some collectors make specific distinction between each type, all in all they were intended for the same purpose, that of carrying something. Early examples which stood upon a foot were used to carry the goblet by one of the under-servants. This form is generally referred to as a tazza. They were usually circular and quite plain, some being decorated on their rims. Later specimens have more complicated decoration. Tazzas made during the latter part of the 17th century might also be engraved with *chinoiseries*. Others might have an engraved border of birds, flowers and foliage. These were followed by another plain period, with perhaps gadrooning on the outer border, the foot also bearing matching gadrooning. The central foot was superseded in about 1715 by three or four feet, usually scroll, bun or shell shaped. By now the tazza was in more general domestic use, and apart from the original purpose for offering drinks, would be used by servants for carrying small objects, letters or documents. It is thought that because of their now generally applied purpose, the name waiter evolved.

Although circular salvers were made until about the end of the second decade of the 18th century, the square or rectangular tray, standing on four feet, rapidly gained in fashion during the 1720's. At first this was square with the corners rounded and shaped in various decorative ways. By the 1730's, the circular shape was popular once again, with a moulded, applied border. These borders would be built up from a number of sections, perhaps six or eight times, combining them with rococo decoration and gadrooning. Many of the salvers during this period were very fine, and designs included very unusual examples, highly decorated in the florid style of the era. Some of these superlative salvers or waiters, as mentioned in the chapter on kettles, were very similar to the stands for kettles. Border designs generally were rather like the tops of contemporary mahogany tripod tables, sometimes referred to as piecrust.

By the middle of the 18th century a variety of shapes was being made, many with hand-raised irregularly shaped rims as well as those with separately cast rims. But whatever sort of rim the tray possessed, one thing is certain: it was almost bound to be enriched at the border either by the applied motifs so beloved during the rococo period, like shells, scrolls, dolphins and masks, or with embossed patterns and hand piercing. Decoration also gradually appeared on the surface of the tray, with all-over chasing forming a pattern quite often around a central space which could be used for a coat-of-arms.

Neo-classical influences made themselves felt during the 1760's, reflected by the use of swags, ribbons, wheat ears, rams' heads and other classical motifs. Not unexpectedly, semi-factory methods also crept into the manufacture of trays. By about 1775, a lot of the round and oval trays were raised with a drop stamp by manufacturing silversmiths, and then finished and decorated elsewhere. A decline in the quality of the rims became thus apparent, and gone for ever was the marvellous variety of decoration found on borders of early examples. Instead, the rims were commonly decorated by gadrooning, beading or reeding, sometimes with a certain amount of added adornment in neo-classical context. While hoof, ball-and-claw and other naturalistically inspired feet supported the tray up till the middle of the 18th century, after this volute feet became fashionable. As with other pieces of tea silver, ball feet were used from the last decade.

During the 18th century the tray had become a vital part of the tea equipage, and upon it would be arranged a glittering array of all that was needed for the sophisticated hostess to infuse the aromatic brew. Thus, the tray needed to be of sufficiently broad dimensions to support the many items of tea silver, including tea pot, tea canisters, sugar bowl and jug. Often such trays measured up to two feet in diameter, and were raised on four small feet as with the smaller versions. Their rims and general decoration were likewise similar. Occasionally they would rest on a wooden stand. Early specimens were circular, but they developed into a more elliptical shape during the neo-classical period. Rims were applied and strengthened with beading; others might be pierced with vertical pales. To these would be attached current decorative motifs. Hand-grips also appeared on some trays at about this time. By the first decade of the 19th century the rim had become far wider, with clumsy gadrooning accompanying the thread edge, now framing revived rococo decoration. Ten years later the tray had become rectangular, commonly embellished with a confusion of busy, chased decoration. Rims were also over-indulged in this respect, and mounts likewise were cast in an amazing assortment of shapes.

Early 18th century American tazzas and salvers were hardly distinguishable from their English counterparts. They were produced both in New York and Boston, and stood upon a supporting foot which was likely to be decorated by gadrooning to match the edge of the tray. Succeeding fashions also followed those set by London silversmiths, with little variation in shape or decoration until about the turn of the 19th century.

Other miscellaneous items which appeared during the last thirty years or so of the 18th century included the cake slice, the delightful beehive honey pots, and butter dishes.

CHAPTER EIGHT

VICTORIAN TEA SILVER

*"There is a great deal of poetry and fine
sentiment in a chest of tea."*

R. W. *Emerson*

To differentiate between Victorian silver and antique silver, it
is essential to know exactly what merits the term "antique". This
is used to denote anything which was made before 1830; before
mass-production and factory methods finally ousted the hand-
made object.

We have traced the development in style of silver tea equipage
to the revival of 18th century rococo which was embarked upon
with so much enthusiasm during the first two decades or so of the
19th century; even before the reign of William IV the Romantic
movement began to influence ornament and decoration, thus the
Victorian era was entered upon on the crest of an exuberant,
uninhibited wave, vulnerable to the unending sequence of exaggerated revivals and quasi-classical styles which were to follow.

The Victorians loved their silver. If they could not afford the
real thing, they contented themselves with as much Sheffield or
electro-plate as their means would allow. Silver was one of the
most important status symbols of the period; the more heavily
decorated the better. Neither was there anything exceptional in
this craving for the metal. As discussed in earlier chapters, it had
long been regarded as a natural means of displaying affluence. The
Victorians cannot, therefore, be singled out for their attitude.

Many of the shapes and styles so popular during the earlier years
of the 19th century, and preceding eras, began to develop during
the early years of Queen Victoria's reign. The base of the familiar
pyriform outline, with its rounded curves, now began to deepen,
becoming broader. The rim, too, widened and this took on wavy

contours, while the handles, cover, stem and foot became enveloped in a mass of decorative foliage.

Although the urn shape, mentioned throughout earlier chapters, was still popular to a certain extent, curvaceous forms echoing the rococo shapes of the mid-18th century retained their place in the world of fashion. There was also the baluster-shaped vessel, which although basically derived from the early 18th century outline, was generally far heavier, with high shoulders and elongated, slender sides, which curved out quite gracefully at the feet.

Whatever the basic shape of the vessel, overall there would be an encrustment of decoration and ornament, so lavishly applied as to completely overwhelm, in most cases, any style of outline. This applied to all pieces of tea silver, including tea pots, milk jugs, tea urns, and particularly the tea kettle. So enamoured were the Victorians of decoration, that they even went so far as to seize on the delightful, simple unadorned pieces of earlier generations, and embellish these, too, with a profusion of ornament. All collectors should be aware of this, and to avoid, if possible buying pieces which have been decorated at a later period.

The British were not the only ones with this fanatical zest for decoration. In America from 1830 onwards the vast areas of expansion, resulting in increased wealth and the unprecedented burst of middle class affluence, meant that the demand for domestic silver reached amazing heights which could only be satisfied by mass-production. At the same time, anything simple or deprived of ornament seemed to be totally abhorred. Like the 19th century middle class of England, Americans generally shunned simplicity. It was almost, one would think, equated in their minds with the lack of personal achievement; the heavy layers of decoration emphasing the owner's prosperity. To make matters worse, in addition to the profuse decoration, the classical shapes borrowed from preceding ages were usually quite unfeelingly modified, producing a jarring confliction of line and form.

American revived styles followed roughly those currently fashionable in England. Included among these were the Empire period, the rococo and the Renaissance, culminating towards the end of the century in *Art Nouveau*. There were also others of less importance. This was the age of the great imitators. Thus, running parallel with the main revivals was an astonishing agglomeration of others embracing Gothic, Elizabethan and Greek forms. Although the copying of styles is not necessarily to be discouraged, since there is nothing aesthetically wrong in doing so, it was the corruption of form, style and decoration which resulted in such artistic abuse.

While decorative themes were borrowed from an assortment of periods, with many evolving from the 18th century and Regency era, two in particular came in for extra attention, namely the acanthus and the vine. The early Victorians exaggerated both in their wild enthusiasm for the naturalistic. On many pieces of tea silver of this time it is quite common, therefore, to find branches and leaves entwining each other, bearing heavy bunches of grapes, mingled with more leaves, convolvulus or even periwinkle plants, leaving the eye in a state of total confusion. Rococo scrolls and flowers were similarly employed. Naturalism reached the apex of its popularity during the 1840's and the following ten years or so, often mingling the bizarre with the vulgar, and incorporating, about this time, exotic plants from the tropics. Thus palm trees became popular, appropriately arranged around Arabs and camels, and evolving into the Moorish style, which was also much beloved in America where it was produced, at a later stage, with characteristic vigour.

The other successful styles, including Elizabethan, Gothic and Renaissance, are distinguished by the following characteristics. The first of the trio made itself apparent mostly by the heavy strapwork which became increasingly popular, commonly found around oval cartouches, and tea silver bore special evidence of Elizabethan-style engraving. The Gothic idiom expressed itself in ideas derived from such architectural ideas as pointed arches and relevant ornamental effects, and was widely used for tea and coffee sets, as well as other sundry objects like toast racks. Among artists whose designs derived from Gothic inspiration was the distinguished designer, A. W. N. Pugin, who influenced style in England and America. His designs were produced by Rundell, Bridge and Rundell and also by John Hardman and Co. Although they were mostly for ecclesiastical works, these influenced domestic silver, especially that used for tea, which took on a distinct aura of formal, Gothic dignity. Renaissance silver, which derived from ideas used by Italian craftsmen, relied for its decorative effect on

88

casting and the addition of flat chasing and engraving. Smaller pieces, like those used at the tea table, were often engraved only, or pierced, as in the case of cake baskets. Towards the middle of the century embossing or *repoussé* work was revived and became very popular.

Confusing are the names of two styles, Louis Quatorze and Louis Quinze. They are generally used to describe certain formal decoration copied from the 18th century; rococo scrolls and floral motifs might thus be mingled with ideas from French designers. It is difficult to specify exact periods for either, but both were extremely popular in England and America. The classical Greek revival, which drew indiscriminately upon anything of Grecian or Etruscan origin, appeared towards the middle of the century and took its place amid the general welter of revivals.

At the Great Exhibition of 1851, examples of such pieces were admired by the thousands who visited the exhibition. Among the tea silver was a dignified tea and coffee service in the Gothic style, richly engraved with a stylised series of patterns, shown by Elkingtons. The kettle greatly resembled the actual shape of a Gothic-style church window, particularly when its pointed oval handle was in an upright position.

In 1845, Sir Henry Cole won the prize which was offered by the Society of Arts for the design of a tea service. Henry Cole held the view that public taste would be uplifted if established sculptors or painters could be inspired to design ordinary domestic objects, which could then be taken up commercially and manufactured on a wide scale. Evolving from such views, also expressed by others, were ideas for some sort of an exhibition at which good design could be on show. The Great Exhibition of 1851, on whose executive committee Henry Cole sat, finally set the seal on these promotional ideas. The commercial success of the Great Exhibition was so immense that others quickly followed: the New York Exhibition of 1853; Dublin, 1853; Paris, 1855; another in London, 1862; the International Centennial Exhibition at Philadelphia, 1876; and the World's Columbian Exposition at Chicago, 1893.

The success of Henry Cole's design for a tea service was one factor which led to the formation two years later of Felix Summerley's Art Manufactures. Felix Summerley was a pseudonym which was used by Cole. This organisation consisted of artists, designers and manufacturers working together to produce work under the general embracing title of Summerley's Art Manufactures. A circular declared that its aim was "to revive the good old practice of connecting the best art with familiar objects in everyday use". Established names connected with the venture included the sculptor John Bell, the painter John Linnell, and the painter and lexicographer, Richard Redgrave.

Silver and silver-plated goods were made for Felix Summerley by Broadhead and Atkin, James Dixon and Sons and Joseph Rodgers and Sons (cutlery) of Sheffield, and by the London firm of Benjamin Smith. John Bell and Richard Redgrave were the two main contributors of metalwork design. Redgrave's "Camellia" tea pot made in silver, silver-plate or Britannia metal by the Sheffield firm of James Dixon and Sons boasts a fairy of Oriental origin gazing at the tea-plant which was made in Parian porcelain by Mintons, the firm which also produced the tea service by Henry Cole which won the Society of Arts prize. Other designs included a tea caddy spoon decorated with the tea-plant by Harry Rogers and produced in both silver and electro-plate. Although this well-intentioned venture succeeded to a certain extent, it also revealed quite clearly at least one important point: namely, that all designers and artists should have a decent knowledge of the materials in which they intend to work. In this the Summerley scheme fell short. The designers produced prototypes intended to be made both in ceramics and metal; sometimes such designs were hardly sympathetic to both. The milk jug of Cole's prize-winning tea service, for instance, was made not only in porcelain by Mintons, but also in silver (with a gilt handle) as well as in glass.

With the great increase in wealth and affluence of the Victorian middle classes, and the resultant growth in demand for domestic silver, there sprang into existence numerous manufacturing firms of silversmiths to cater for the unprecedented demand both in England and America. Mass-production methods, evolving from the embryonic developments of the late 18th century, meant that not only an incredible amount of sterling silver but also a vast range of plated goods now found its way into homes everywhere.

The famous firm of Hunt and Roskell had a strong link with the great Regency silversmith, Paul Storr, who had worked for Rundell, Bridge and Rundell during the first two decades of the 19th century. From this time he acquired his own premises in Harrison Street, off Gray's Inn Lane, and this firm after various changes became Hunt and Roskell, which name it retained until 1897. A year later it was bought by J. W. Benson.

Philip Rundell, another prominent Regency personality, was in partnership at the sign of the "Golden Salmon" on Ludgate Hill. John Bridge, their principal maker, joined them in about 1780, and the firm of Rundell, Bridge and Rundell prospered to such an extent that by the first decade of the 19th century they were employing as many as a thousand hands, with order books overflowing. Thus, collectors stand a good chance of finding silver by this firm because of the enormous amount which was produced, including a variety of tea pieces. Despite their big staff, Rundell, Bridge and Rundell still could not keep abreast of demand, and because of this they passed on certain commissions to other firms, including Digby Scott and Benjamin Smith, who entered their mark in 1802, or to Paul Storr. Among the leading designers used by Rundell's were Francis Chantrey (1781–1841); John Flaxman (1756–1834); the younger Charles Catton (1756–1819); and William Theed (1764–1817).

Hancocks was founded in Bruton Street, London, towards the middle of the 19th century by Charles Frederick Hancock. Smith and Nicholson of Duke Street, Lincoln's Inn Fields, was descended from the Regency silversmith Benjamin Smith, already mentioned. Benjamin Smith, the son, succeeded as head of the firm which became known as Smith & Nicholson from 1850 to 1865, after which it was known as Stephen Smith. Another well-known London firm was J. Angell of the Strand, whose tea services included some amazing shapes decorated with extreme patterns of rococo scrolls and Elizabethan strapwork. Important Sheffield firms included Broadhead and Atkin, who showed a lobed-shaped tea and coffee set at the Great Exhibition, decorated with naturalistic flowers, with feet and handles shaped like rustic branches; Thomas Bradbury and Sons, who exhibited a tea and coffee set modelled from the pitcher plant; James Dixon and Sons; and Hawkesworth, Eyre and Co.

The famous Birmingham firm of Elkington also came into being during the 19th century. Like many of the firms mentioned, they figured prominently in the display of silver at the Great Exhibition, although many of their products were electro-plated, a process which is dealt with in another chapter. Tea services in the decorative styles current at the time won loud acclaim. Other Birmingham firms included G. R. Collis; T. Wilkinson and Company, who produced a tea urn in the form of an Etruscan vase, decorated with beading and applied palmettes on the rim, handle and tap, and mounted on a rocky base on which sat two children playing musical instruments; Prime and Son; and Cartwright and Hirons, showing, among other pieces, cake baskets decorated with vine leaves, salvers incorporating Elizabethan strapwork and toast racks with scroll work.

Thus by the mid-1850's, factory methods, adequately geared for continuous mass-production, were efficiently churning out an overwhelming variety of tea silver in an equally wide variety of prices. While for many years collectors have remained disinterested generally in such pieces, the tables have now turned full scale, and Victoriana has become as collectable as work from other periods, with a corresponding rise in all prices. Many of the items once despised as being vulgar or overdecorated, are now eagerly sought by collectors. This change of attitude embraces not only Victorian tea silver inspired by past fashions, but also those pieces influenced by the fluid lines of *Art Nouveau* which emerged towards the end of the 19th century.

During the eleven years between the Great Exhibition of 1851 and the International Exhibition which was held in 1862, the passion for naturalistic design gradually waned. Such are the caprices of fashion that it was toppled from popularity by an old favourite, the classical form. Naturalism had provoked much criticism from artists and designers, but because of its popularity and its proven commercial value, manufacturers were loathe to replace it with anything else, although, towards the middle of the century, naturalistic motifs were often less lavishly applied, but not in all cases, and Moorish inspired naturalism was still extremely popular. Likewise, the revived rococo style, also of long-standing appeal, now began to play a less prominent role, although some smaller firms still retained this style and doggedly continued in their mass-production of it. The Elizabethan style continued to be popular, as did Gothic pieces, but neither had had such an immense following as naturalism and rococo.

The new forms of decoration were based on classical and Renaissance origins. Classical shapes and ornament now cascaded on to the market, commonly described as Etruscan, Pompeian or just plain Greek. A much favoured shape for certain types of jug was the Greek "oenochoe" (the classical urn shape of the Greek vessel used for filling the cups with wine), and a form based on this was used for tea pots, milk jugs and spherical sugar bowls on a moulded stem and foot. It was joined by various other classical shapes similar to those employed during the neo-classical period of the 18th century. After the ostentation of naturalism, decoration now oscillated to the extremes of simplicity. Ornament became very restrained, and, surprisingly, thoroughly correct, subservient to the form. As with 18th century pieces, two of the most common types of decoration were beading and engraving, although the latter was generally of intricate scenes, perhaps depicting Greek soldiers or chariots and horses. Such a scene would be contained in a stylised border of appropriate classical motifs. This tender respect for classicism did not last, however, and gradually the shapes became less pure; the outlines veering towards the exaggerated, with ornate naturalistic decoration becoming abundant.

The other decorative style, that of the Renaissance, embraced acanthus leaves, lions', rams' and goats' masks, and the heads of griffins and sphinxes. Engraved and chased ornament of strapwork was used in close combination with stylised foliage and scrolls.

At the International Exhibition of 1862 appeared a strange miscellanea of styles; tea and coffee services in the Greek style, with elegant urn-shaped vessels, decorated by fluting, the key design or ovolo borders; services in the Renaissance style, embellished with scrolls and rock motifs; tea pots in the Elizabethan idiom with strapwork and elaborate cartouches; and all sorts of tea equipage influenced by Gothic aspirations, including mouldings, trefoils, formal vine leaves and ropework. Critics were kindly disposed towards the exhibition, and it was generally agreed that there had been definite progress in art since the Great Exhibition of 1851. Such a consensus of opinion may seem strange to enlightened souls of the 20th century, but no doubt all those concerned were expressing perfectly sincere beliefs. However, more important was the fact that out of this agglomeration of borrowed styles there now appeared more clearly defined characteristics to usher in the new designs of the 1860's.

Angular shapes and styles began to appear, sometimes emphasised by decoration. Tea pots, for example, would often have their rounded sides sloping down and outwards at quite a pronounced angle to the flat base, just before which they turned inward at an opposing angle. The Greek "oenochoe" shape had evolved into round-bodied vessels, decorated by hands of moulding, occasionally with an elongated neck and high trefoil lips. Tall, uncompromising handles, reaching well above the tea pot, became popular. These might be straight-sided and angular, complementing the shape of the vessel. By the 1870's handles tended to be better balanced. They had become wider at the top, meeting the upward swing of the handle at a sharp angle. The general effect, whether one liked it or not, was altogether more modern, since it strove to break away from the resurrected outlines of previous centuries.

Even so, old habits die hard, and such new ideas did not by any means sweep the board. A constant following remained for late 18th century styles, and there were some designs shown in the 1862 Exhibition which had been copied almost exactly from Adam forms. A modified form of three-dimensional naturalism was also retained, particularly as far as more important pieces were concerned, and Elizabethan, Moorish and rococo influences lingered on for some time. During the 1860's the over-exuberant cast and applied relief decoration was gradually susperseded by engraving and flat chasing. Particularly popular were engraved classical scenes and motifs, derived from the key design and ovolo. Egyptian, Persian and Indian patterns also enjoyed a certain amount of popularity. The copies of late 18th century classical styles which had been apparent at the exhibition became more fashionable during the 1870's, and with them came all the accompanying decorative effects typical of the period.

A new influence came from Japan. Displays of Japanese art which had been held in London in 1862 had received a great deal of attention, resulting in a positive mania for Japanese styles and decoration. During the 1870's engravings of Japanese birds and plants might appear on tea services in much the same way as *chinoiseries* embellished mid-18th century work. Modified Japanese shapes were later employed for the actual vessel, together with imitation bamboo handles.

The term Louis Seize was used for styles which were derived from various shapes popular during the last two or three decades of the 18th century, and even worse, "Queen Anne" became an all-embracing description not only for styles copied from early 18th century ideas, but many more made long after this period.

Tea pots originating from late 18th century outlines were straight-sided, tapering towards the shoulders, usually oval or oblong and slightly lobed. Handles were commonly based on the scroll, embellished with acanthus foliage, perhaps fluted, but quite often also plain and flat-topped. Spouts might be either straight or slightly curved and fluted. By the following decade fashions veered towards shapes derived from the Regency period, being generally squat and rounded. Tea services based on these shapes were far less elegant. The graceful "Queen Anne" outline continued in fashion, embracing the numerous latter forms.

By the last twenty years of the 19th century, therefore, there was still much simulation of style; all of which was proving a most viable commercial proposition. Manufacturing silversmiths and retailers alike were well pleased with things as they were; not so the artists and designers of the period. The visual arts had become increasingly impoverished through the years, the amount of copying and imitation having a stultifying effect generally. From this state of sloth there gradually appeared a new movement, the fluid, simple lines of which stood out in contrast to anything else being produced at the time. *Art Nouveau* was the name given to the new movement, and the time of its emergence varied slightly from country to country. Generally speaking, although in some cases it was earlier, it began to make itself felt around the last decade of the century, coming roughly to its final years with the advent of the First World War. Not all countries come under its influence, and where it did become popular not all artists and designers subscribed to the new school of thought. Nevertheless, its impact was important in many quarters, although, sadly, many of the prototypes which were produced for silver never saw the light of day commercially. *Art Nouveau* was an interesting mixture of oriental-

and medieval-inspired ideas, at its best beautifully expressed in gentle, flowing lines which some people found hard to appreciate after the uncompromising reproductions and imitations of the 19th century. By the turn of the century, several firms were producing domestic silver in the new style, including Elkingtons. Others produced modified versions. Individual designers also produced a great deal of fine work.

Among these was Charles Robert Ashbee (1863–1942), who trained originally as an architect and was an ardent follower of William Morris. Ashbee believed that truly good design and craftsmanship could not come from the mechanical or the industrial organisations. He applied this thought particularly to the silversmith's craft, and in 1887 founded the School and Guild of Handicraft, which survived until 1908. During its first years, the Guild produced much silver which carried Ashbee's own initials by the side of the hall-mark. Ashbee was the Guild's chief designer and he trained the workmen himself, most of whom had no previous experience of silversmithing, although they quickly came to be expert at the craft. He was adamant in his opinion that a piece of silver could only be good if it had "feeling and character". He also demanded that each craftsman, whatever their particular contribution to a piece, should have an appreciation of the piece as a whole. He believed in the small workshop where the craftsmen were familiar with each other's methods. They must all possess a knowledge of traditional methods. In fact, Ashbee was endeavouring to return to the original state of the craft before mechanical innovations made possible mass-production towards the end of the 18th century.

Ashbee abhorred the barren creative fields of commercialism and longed instead to inject the silver which his Guild produced with feeling and individuality. This he succeeded in doing. The silver produced in his workshop abounds with character. Beaten up from the flat (the surface of pieces usually bears evidence of the hammer), it has a delightful, soft sheen about it, utterly in contrast to the harsh metallic tones of commercially produced pieces. Tea services made by the Guild, not unnaturally, were based on either the urn shape or the pear shape, being very simple and beautiful; sugar bowls had unassuming moulded edges and wide wire handles. Ashbee made much use of silver wires in his

34. Pierced Adam-style bread basket by Charles Aldridge and Henry Green, 1774. (J. H. Bourdon-Smith Ltd.)

35. A George I sugar caster by Paul de Lamerie, 1725. (Garrard and Company Ltd.)

36. George II Irish casters, Dublin, c. 1737. (Sotheby)

37. Casters, top, left to right: by George Giles, his mark overstamping the Bateman mark of 1792; by Thomas Satchwell made in 1791; by Robert Peaston, 1771. Bottom, left to right: by Sam Wood, 1762; an earlier example by Sam Wood, 1748; a John Delmester caster of 1762, with a flattish bun top; a 1773 bun top example by J. and T. Daniel. (J. H. Bourdon-Smith Ltd.)

38. A Queen Anne tazza made by William Andrews in 1703. (J. H. Bourdon-Smith Ltd.)

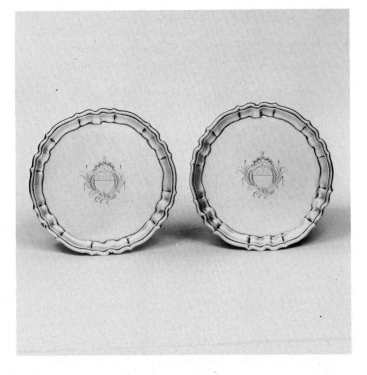

39. A pair of waiters, engraved with the contemporary arms of Harrison, by David Wilks, 1737. (J. H. Bourdon-Smith Ltd.)

40. Made by Paul de Lamerie in 1725, this George I waiter has an engraved coat-of-arms and stylised decoration. (Sotheby)

41. An Irish octafoil waiter with a raised border, engraved with a contemporary coat-of-arms within a formal scroll, foliate and strapwork cartouche, by Thomas Slade, Dublin, 1725. (Sotheby)

42. A George III silver galleried tray, made in London in 1801.

43. A Victorian salver made in 1838 by H. Wilkinson and Company in Sheffield, decorated with grape and vine leaf motif around the border, and finely chased within. (J. H. Bourdon-Smith Ltd.)

work, characteristic uses being twisted wire finials and supporting arched wires beneath bowls. His sugar casters reflected the ideas of the late 17th century and were usually cylindrical in shape like these early examples.

Another great exponent of the ideas of William Morris was W. A. S. Benson (1854–1924), who designed and produced metal-work on a commercial scale during the 1880's. He opened his shop in Bond Street in 1887, but unlike Ashbee his purpose was to prove that methods used commercially could also be employed to produce good design. He produced some fine tea silver, includ-ing simple, spun shapes of functional but aesthetic proportions.

Omar Ramsden (1873–1939) also built a reputation for pur-poseful yet pleasing work of a high calibre. Gilbert Marks (1861–1905) became fashionable in the 1890's, and exhibited many of his pieces including pear-shaped jugs, broad-flanged dishes and trays.

Various Guilds sprang up around the country, based generally on Ashbee's ideas. One of the most notable was that founded by Arthur Dixon (1856–1929) at Birmingham. Again the silver that came from this workshop was simple and usually undecorated, hammered up from the flat, with forged handles joined to the body in a graceful curve.

In America, Tiffany and Company of New York produced some superlative work designed by followers of the *Art Nouveau* movement. It embraced all types of silver for a wide range of purposes, including tea silver, vases and personal items like buckles and trinkets. While some are considered to be among the finest examples of *Art Nouveau*, there are others including various tea and coffee sets which to a certain extent fall short of the necessary fine-ness characteristically essential to the style. Nevertheless, much of the work produced by designers for Tiffany and Company during this period was of such a high calibre as to result in the name of that organisation becoming almost synonymous with the move-ment during the era.

CHAPTER NINE

SHEFFIELD PLATE

*" Tea, though ridiculed by those who are naturally coarse
in their nervous sensibilities . . . will always be the
favourite beverage of the intellectual."*

Thomas de Quincey

Today, not everybody can afford to collect old silver. During the
18th century few could afford to buy it for any reason. Even when
new factory methods made it more generally available towards the
end of the 18th century, there was still a large proportion of the
population who would never know the delights of such a luxury.

However, there was one way in which those with more modest
means might avail themselves of a set of silver tea equipage. In
about 1742, a Sheffield cutler named Thomas Boulsover made an
important discovery which was soon to lead to the lustre of silver
shining forth from many an ordinary man's table.

He found that it was possible to fuse by heat a sheet of silver on
to a thicker piece of copper. When both metals fused as one were
rolled, they then expanded to become a thin sheet of copper
coated with a layer of silver. To begin with Thomas Boulsover
made his new plated copper into buttons, boxes and various other
small objects, all of which were far less expensive than their
counterparts in silver. As far as appearances were concerned, they
looked very similar.

Within about ten years Boulsover's discovery was taken up by
other manufacturers and gradually became one of Sheffield's most
lucrative industries. In particular, Joseph Hancock exploited
Boulsover's discovery, and from about the mid-1750's began to
manufacture a variety of domestic articles with the new silver-
coated copper.

Sheffield plate, however, as the new process came to be known, did not long remain the sole industry of the town from which its name originated. Matthew Boulton, that energetic manufacturer of metal goods from Birmingham, was quick to see the potential of the new technique and made a point of visiting Sheffield to learn about the process. By 1762, he went into production of Sheffield plate at his Soho, Birmingham, factory. Not only was Boulton a genius with metal, his business acumen appeared to equal his creativity. Very quickly he obtained a monopoly of the manufacture of Sheffield plate in Birmingham, thus becoming the most important single manufacturer outside of Sheffield itself. The pieces to come from Boulton's factory during these years were among the best of their kind, and other manufacturers soon began to copy his work.

The rolling-mill, already fully discussed in previous chapters, was also used in the rolling of Sheffield plate. Early plate was only silver-coated on one side, but after about the mid 1760's new methods enabled the copper to be coated on both sides, and this meant that the rolled plate was virtually indistinguishable from silver.

Although Sheffield plate was inexpensive, there was nothing sub-standard about either its methods of production or its quality. From the beginning manufacturers were most assiduous in their efforts to combat the many technical difficulties naturally inherent in the new plate. They worked hard to perfect the finished article, either employing the new processes in use towards the end of the 18th century by silversmiths, or carefully adapting them to suit the idiosyncrasies encountered in the production of the new plated goods. Soon manufacturers were producing really fine pieces, and at a price which many could afford. By the mid-1780's, for example, a tea pot made in Sheffield plate would probably cost about a third of the price of its silver counterpart.

An important discovery later made possible the plating of copper wire. Fine strips of silver were coated around copper rods and then united by heat fusion, similar to the actual plate. The fused rods were then passed through an instrument which left it as "silver" wire.

Although it is considered attractive today to be able to see some of the copper gleaming through the silver on genuine old Sheffield plate (where the coating of silver has worn thin over the years), a condition usually referred to as "bleeding", in the 18th century the unwanted glow of copper on vessels was the bane of manufacturers' lives. For many years after Sheffield plate had first been discovered, the copper could be discerned along the edges of vessels. Manufacturers now welcomed the new coated wire as one way of solving the problem. This was placed along the edges and thus concealed the unwanted colour of the copper.

In about 1785 Samuel Roberts and George Cadman perfected a further method, using sterling silver wire to conceal the copper. Matthew Boulton's plated wares were fine examples of the new method, some of which bear the added inscription "Silver Borders" upon them. Sheffield manufacturers also drew attention to the innovation, adding the description "Silver Edges" on their products. Also made of silver were the shields let into the plate for the engraving of coats-of-arms. This was necessary as it was quite impossible to engrave a plated surface with the usual amount of silver on it; the copper would immediately be revealed by the craftsman's instrument. The technique of rubbing-in silver shields was discovered in about 1810. Before this, such shields were made of heavily plated sections and soldered into place.

From about 1820, hollow-ware was shaped by lathe-spinning. The rolled sheet of plated copper was forced on to a wooden chuck of the necessary shape, which was then revolved. This was a quicker method than die-stamping. Sometimes you can detect the pieces made by this method by closely examining the interiors for traces of the spiralling pressure which was applied.

In 1830 another plating process was developed. Samuel Roberts took out a patent which enabled the introduction of a layer of German silver (later to be called nickel silver) or other white metal alloy between the silver coating and the copper. This meant that when the actual silver wore away, it would reveal the silver-toned alloy and not the copper. The alloy was of nickel, copper and zinc, brought from Berlin, and at first it was too brittle to be used to replace the copper. Within about six years an improved version known as Argentine had become available, and this quickly superseded copper. Because of the silver colour of the alloy, it became unnecessary to use such a heavy coating of silver, and in order to lessen the cost of the end product still further, manufacturers used less and less of the precious metal. The economics of the exercise were of the utmost importance at the time because of the influx of cheap, plated goods from France, and also because of competition in the export market. Although the French products were inferior to the British wares, they had the advantage of being far less expensive. The copper was of a deeper shade, and the silver coating was extremely thin. In order to keep costs to an absolute minimum, refinements like silver edges were hardly ever used on such pieces.

Practically all the designs and shapes popular in silver could be copied in Sheffield plate, and manufacturers were prolific in their output of all pieces of tea equipage. Such firms were often changing their names as partners left and new ones joined, or larger manufacturers took over smaller concerns. Many of them also made silver goods, and this flood of machine-made silver and plate from Sheffield and Birmingham became a dangerous challenge to older methods and techniques, in the end completely eclipsing them. The important Sheffield firms producing plated silver included Thomas Bradbury & Sons, James Dixon and Sons, T. and J. Creswick, I. and I. Waterhouse and Company, Padley, Parkin and Company, Henry Wilkinson and Company, Roberts, Smith and Company (to become Smith, Sissons and Company in 1848), Gainsford and Nicholson and Hawkesworth, Eyre and Company. In Birmingham, the Soho works was still the most important producer of Sheffield plate. By 1837 the firm was known as Matthew Robinson Boulton (the son of the first Matthew), who died in 1842 when the firm passed on to his son, M. P. W. Boulton. In 1848, the firm closed and the dies were sold.

Some Sheffield plate bears distinguishing marks, although it was illegal to mark Sheffield plate between 1773 to 1784, so similar had become the marks to hall-marks. The earliest record of a mark can be traced back to the time when Joseph Hancock first went into production around 1755. His initial punch is not dissimilar to that used by contemporary London silversmiths. Sadly, no mark seems to have been traced for the inventor of Sheffield plate, Thomas Boulsover. Other early punches include the initials NS for Nathanial Smith (1756); TL for Thomas Law, also Tho. Law in full (1758); T L for Tudor and Leader (1760); B & F for Boulton and Fothergill (1764); J S R for Jacob and Samuel Roberts (1765); IW for John Winter and Company

(1765); M.Co for Richard Morton (1765); I R for J. Rowbotham and Company (1768); A E Co for Ashforth, Ellis and Company; and J.L PLATED for J. Littlewood (1772).

By the year 1784, Sheffield plate manufacturers were again authorised to mark their wares, this time with some sort of emblem and the maker's name, although such marks were not to resemble those found on silver goods. Despite this, some manufacturers continued to use marks which could be mistaken for hallmarks. The new marks had to be registered at the assay offices, if manufacturers wished to use them. Unfortunately, many producers of Sheffield plate did not bother, which means that there is much unmarked plate still in existence.

In addition to their own marks, a crown was quite commonly used between 1765 and 1825 to denote quality. Among others, it appeared on wares made by John Winter and Company, E. Thomason and Dowler, T. Law and Company, I. and I. Waterhouse and Company, Pemberton and Mitchell, W. Briggs and J. Willmore. From a collector's point of view it is worth remembering this device and five others, namely the bell, the open hand, the crossed arrows, the pineapple and the crossed keys, since to confuse matters still further, they all appeared on some electroplated items at a later stage. In fact, the use of the crown to denote quality was becoming far too confusing in the 19th century, and it was eventually prohibited in 1896.

The open hand was used, among others, by N. Smith and Company from about 1784; Smith, Tate, Nicholson and Hoult from about 1810; J. Watson and Son from about 1830; and Padley, Parkin and Company from about 1840. Those using the bell included Roberts, Cadman and Company from about 1785; Roberts, Smith and Company from about 1828; and Smith, Sissons and Company from about 1848. The firm of T. and J. Creswick used the crossed arrows device (1811), while H. Wilkinson and Company employed the crossed keys symbol (1836). Generally speaking, however, distinguishing emblems used by Sheffield plate manufacturers were as diverse as the objects they produced and included, among others, a globe and cross (Hawkesworth, Eyre and Company), a ram's head (Froggatt, Coldwell and Lean) and W. Coldwell, a bishop's mitre (S. and C. Younge and Co.), a ship in full sail (Watson, Fenton and Bradbury), and an open umbrella (Tonks and Company). Thus the whole system of marking Sheffield plate was unreliable in the extreme, and when German silver was introduced, closely followed by its improved version, some manufacturers reverted to their original tendency of making the marks resemble as closely as possible those used on sterling silver. Although London silversmiths had managed to obtain an injunction restraining Sheffield plate manufacturers from using such marks in 1773, nothing further was done when the really cheap plated goods flooded the market during the following century. Because of this it always pays to give more than a cursory glance at any marks, however convincing and similar to hall-marks they may at first appear.

Sheffield plate ruled supreme for roughly a century, from about 1742 until the introduction of German silver. All pieces of tea silver were produced in it, although as the years went by Sheffield plated goods tended to lag a little behind the fashions. This is particularly apparent in tea services, which were ensured of constant sales, and therefore, manufacturers felt, did not necessitate the expense of too many new dies. For instance, the melon-shaped tea pot remained popular in Sheffield plate for longer than its silver counterpart. Rococo ornament continued to embellish tea services, and the popular lobed shapes maintained their appeal. As so much was produced in Sheffield plate, the collector has a great deal from which to choose, and at one time could have done so for very little outlay. Today, however, prices of good plate have risen, although there are still bargains to be found. The main problem when building up a collection of Sheffield plate is, of course, the inadequacy of the marking system, added to which it has been copied extensively in more recent years. The standard book for information on old Sheffield plate is Frederick Bradbury's *History of Old Silver Plate*, which illustrates some of the marks used by manufacturers. Frederick Bradbury (a member of the Bradbury family) also compiled an invaluable pocket-size book, *British and Irish Silver Assay Office Marks, 1544–1959*, which also contains lists of Sheffield plate marks.

During the final years of the 19th century and later, some firms produced a type of plate simulating old Sheffield plate. These imitations were convincingly produced in copper and electro-plated, often closely resembling early styles. They were described as Sheffield plate and sold as this, but, of course, as they were electro-plated, such a description was inaccurate. In 1911, the Sheffield Cutlers' Company took action and obtained an injunction that the term "Sheffield plate" should not be used for any pieces other than those made by the original method of fusing the silver and the copper.

Although the advent of electro-plating resulted in the swift decline of the Sheffield plate industry, one or two firms continued to produce it, including Thomas Bradbury and Sons, who tried the new method of electro-plating but abandoned it because they were not satisfied. James Dixon and Sons also continued to make Sheffield plate, having shown fine examples at both the Great Exhibition of 1851 and the International Exhibition of 1862. During the latter they received a medal "for the general excellence of their works in Sheffield and electro-plate". Their pieces included tea and coffee services of classical urn shapes, decorated with classical stylised ornament. Although a few firms remained faithful to this old method of plating, most were only too ready to turn over to the cheap, new process of electro-plating. However, even as late as 1878, Sheffield plate made by Ridge, Woodcock and Hardy appeared at the International Exhibition in Paris, although this appearance must really be regarded as a swan song, for the story of Sheffield plate was certainly nearing its final chapters.

From a collector's point of view early Sheffield plate can be most rewarding. Some of the work, particularly the more delicate pieces like cake baskets, was extremely intricate. Sometimes on the better pieces, the feet, handles and mounts would be of thin sheet silver, filled with solder, then shaped to the required form before being soldered on to the object. Unfortunately over the years much old Sheffield plate has been returned to the workshop for re-plating by the cheaper process of electro-deposition. Today, few people would be so unenlightened as to do this, and the mellow tones of the old plate, together with the glow of copper where the silver has worn thin, is appreciated in its own right.

CHAPTER TEN

ELECTRO-PLATE

" Thank God for tea! What would the world
do without tea? How did it exist? I am glad
I was not born before tea."

Sydney Smith

Never to be confused with Sheffield plate is the process of electro-plating. This deserves mention for three important reasons. It replaced Sheffield plate generally; more tea services have probably been produced in electro-plate than have appeared either in silver or Sheffield plate; and thirdly, good electro-plated pieces produced during the 19th century are now gradually becoming collectable.

A patent concerning an entirely new process for coating metals with zinc was applied for as far back as 1838 by G. R. Elkington and O. W. Barratt, and while the patent did not mention the magic word "electricity", it is thought that a single-cell battery was used in the amazing new process.

Until this time all forms of metal working had been carried on with heat from the furnace. The revelation that electricity might now replace the ancient methods using fire caused great excitement.

Many scientists had carried out experiments in electro-metallurgy following Alessandro Volta's invention of an electric battery in 1800, and within five years Brugnatelli had scored a double success by coating two silver medals with gold by electricity. There were still many problems which perplexed scientists, not least of these being the difficulties experienced in obtaining an even deposit over the entire surface of an object. Another concerned the permanent sticking of the deposit to the surface. By the second and third decades of the 19th century, however, progress and new discoveries in the field of electro-metallurgy resulted in the gradual resolving of many of these problems.

A surgeon, by the name of John Wright, seems to have been largely responsible for solving the problem of obtaining the correct adhesive coating for silver. He had been working on the uses of solutions of cyanides of gold and silver in cyanide of potassium from an idea submitted in Scheele's *Chemical Essays*. In 1840 (nearly 100 years after Thomas Boulsover had discovered that it was possible to fuse silver on to copper) John Wright entered into partnership with Elkingtons, selling them his invention in return not only for a sum of money, but also for royalties on all silver deposited, not to mention all licences granted under the patent.

More experiments, however, were needed to perfect the new method, and these continued during the next few years, with further revised patents being applied for by Elkingtons. Included among these was one of great importance, which laid the foundations for making electrotypes of existing pieces, by causing either silver or gold to be deposited by electric means in or on suitable models. A further patent concerned the method of producing a gold design on a silver or other metal surface, done simply by pencilling by hand or by printing from plates or rolls upon paper, any sort of pattern in a suitable stopping varnish. This would then be applied to the object to be decorated, carefully pressed or rubbed and allowed to dry, after which the gold design could be affixed by the electro-process of gilding, the varnish being later removed by turpentine or other chemicals.

Towards the end of the 1840's, a further significant patent was taken out by Elkingtons for a method which involved the addition of sulphur or carbon compounds to the solution of metals which resulted in a far more brilliant surface during the deposition procedure.

Despite the fact that the process of electro-plating as such was new, many of the actual methods of manufacture of wares were the same as those used in the production of Sheffield plate, with one very big difference. Whereas in the manufacture of Sheffield plate the plating of copper with silver had been the first step in the process, the actual sheets of copper being thus coated before they were made into objects, in electro-plating the object was made and decorated first, and then immersed in the plating vat.

Some of the earlier electro-plated pieces were cast in German silver or Britannia Metal, which was an alloy of tin, antimony and copper. However, the main parts of pieces of tea silver were also raised from the flat as of old, and appendages like handles and spouts being mass-produced and then soldered into position. After the middle of the 19th century, big improvements were apparent in the process of stamping, and Elkingtons were the proud possessors of a stamping machine which was powered by steam, and which produced large objects swiftly and efficiently. Further improvements materialised during the following decades.

When a tea pot had been shaped and its spout and handle joined by soldering, the next step would be that of decorating. Engraving was either carried out by hand, or by an alternative process of etching which looked like engraving. Decorating by engine-turning was also commonly employed. Silver-plated wire was used for decoration, as it had been during the preceding century with Sheffield plated wares. Piercing was either mechanically carried out or cut by hand. Finally, the vessel would be placed in the plating vat where it would be coated in silver, to be assiduously tapped all over on its emergence, thus ensuring that the plating was firmly affixed. Women would then add the final effective burnishings.

In many ways electro-plating can be looked upon as the final step in the evolution of tea silver. By its cheapness, the pleasure of owning a silver tea set was at last brought within the reach of everybody. The multifarious designs produced meant that this wide public could now indulge itself to its heart's content when choosing, not only tea silver, but ancillary pieces like trays. At long last the working man, for so long a keen imbiber of tea, could indulge as well in the prestigious ownership of "silver".

By the fourth decade of the 19th century, numerous other firms began to produce electro-plated goods under the licences resulting from Elkingtons' patent rights, and while electro-plating had at first encountered much criticism, this quickly diminished when manufacturers saw its commercial potential based on mass-production. At the Great Exhibition in 1851, the bright glitter of electro-plated goods was much in evidence, and during the following decade or so the process of electro-plating proved so successful that it largely superseded the older methods of plating based on Thomas Boulsover's original conception.

Electro-plating was here to stay. What the rich man had in silver, the ordinary man could afford in the new plate. Manufacturers quite commonly produced the same designs in silver and electro-plate, just as they had done in Sheffield plate during the preceding generation. Electro-plating not only speeded up mechanical processes in the production of silver objects generally, it also influenced naturalistic design. Sometimes, according to the literature of the period, fruit and flowers, even lizards or birds might be given a coating of metal and preserved by immersing them in the plating solution, as an additional guide to the modeller. With the great fashion for naturalism, such achievements were extremely important and much prized.

But electrotype processes were used not only to achieve naturalism. They also played a valuable part in sustaining other art forms including Greek and Roman plate, and also Renaissance works of art. A room at Marlborough House was allocated specifically for the purpose of making electrotypes of the works of art in its museum.

The electro-plated side of Elkingtons' business grew to form the basis of this Birmingham firm's prosperity, enabling them to expand in the following decades, producing works of great artistic merit. As the popularity of the new process increased, so Elkingtons issued more licences to manufacturers not only in Birmingham, but in Sheffield and London. By the middle of the century such licences were available on improved terms, because by then the patent was valid for a shorter period.

Electro-plated tea services, following the fashions current in silver and described in the chapter on Victorian silver, now flooded the market. Much of this 19th century plate, of excellent quality, is still available today, and where 18th century classical styles have been followed in particular, is a worthwhile contribution in its own right.

Although these styles were based largely on preceding fashions, with additions or alterations in design indicative of 19th century influence, the later years of the century also produced much original thought. Christopher Dresser (1834–1904), for example, was among designers whose ingenuity and originality influenced tea silver. He began producing designs for silver in the 1860's, working for Elkingtons, James Dixon and Sons and also Hukin and Heath. His work is usually distinctly functional. Characteristic of this tendency is an electro-plated tea set made by Dixons in 1881. All the pieces have undecorated, spherical bodies, standing on three slender, curved legs with simple feet. The rivets which fix the feet and handles to the bodies are both functional and decorative.

An extreme example of Dresser's obsession with the functional can be seen in a strange electro-plated tea pot made by Dixons at about the same time. Squat, round and with a sliced-off look at the top, this has a small hinged lid which takes up about a quarter of the flat surface, the hinge running across the pot, instead of at the side as usual. The ebony handle is mounted at an alarming angle, and looks as though it is about to be rocketed into space.

Two designs by Dresser for Elkingtons, characteristic of his later work, include a tea pot made of a cylindrical piece of metal, with the top and bottom produced by cutting the edges of the cylinder, bending them inwards and joining with rivets. The edges were left showing, as were the joins of the spout which was in the form of a spiral. The handle was a simple rod-like appendage, parallel with the body and fixed by functional strips of metal. The other design is for a tea pot, cream jug and sugar basin, decorated by mouldings on the lower part of the bodies and on the tea pot lid. Similarly, mouldings also appear on the mouths of the sugar basin and cream jug. In applying them, Dresser has merely repeated the techniques of earlier craftsmen, as far back as the late 17th century, namely of using a form of decoration to strengthen the weak areas of a vessel. Thus, while the development in processes had made great strides, and designers had sought creative progress, the simple, effective means of an earlier age had again proved their worth by being the most realistic.

CHAPTER ELEVEN

HALL-MARKS

The origins of the British hall-marking system can be traced back to the Middle Ages. Collectors of silver can naturally benefit greatly from a sound knowledge of these marks. They have been used in one form or another for hundreds of years, and can enable silver enthusiasts to discover not only where in England the piece was assayed, but also in which year it was made, and often which silversmith actually produced the object.

Because hall-marking is such an ancient and well tested system of regularising the standards of silver, it is essential that all lovers of old silver learn something of its origins. The craft of the goldsmith (the term goldsmith is used in its generic sense) was always highly esteemed, and because of this it is likely that various forms of associations of goldsmiths may have existed long before records were made. One of the first mentions of such a group of craftsmen does not appear until about 1180, and then it was in a detrimental vein. Together with various groups of other craftsmen and tradesmen, goldsmiths were fined for setting up small groups or organisations without the consent of the king.

By 1238, however, things had taken a decided turn for the better. A decree empowered the mayor and aldermen to choose six goldsmiths in the City of London to superintend their craft. The responsibilities of the revered six were to include ensuring that the work was carried out in the public street, and not in secret, and, even more important, because it was the first time that any attempt had been made to regularise the standard of silver and gold, that the silver used should not be worse in fineness than that used for coinage at the Mint. Gold was to be of no colour other than its own and should not be worth less than one hundred shillings for a mark of Tower weight. (The Tower pound was abolished in 1527. It consisted of 5,400 grains Troy and was replaced by the heavier

Troy pound, which had already been in use for several decades. The Troy pound was superseded in 1878 by the Avoirdupois pound, except for weighing precious metals or stones.)

Thus in embryonic form was set out the British hall-marking system. From this decree there stemmed, as time progressed, gradual definitions as to the more specific responsibilities of the goldsmith, whilst at the same time there emerged laws for safe-guards against frauds. By the time Henry VII came to the throne there had become instituted, under the direct control of the gold-smiths themselves, with the full support of the law, a system of regularising the standard of British silver and gold which was unsurpassed throughout the world.

Of very great importance was an Act passed under Edward I in 1300, which refers to the "gardiens". It might almost be described as the first of any movement aimed at consumer protection. The Act ordained that "no goldsmith of England, nor none other where within the King's dominion . . . shall from henceforth make or cause to be made any manner of vessel, jewel or any other thing of gold or silver, except it be of good and true allay, that is to say, gold of a certain touch, and silver of the esterling allay or of better, at the pleasure of him to whom the work belongeth."

The Act added that all objects should be assayed by the "gardiens of the Craft", and that these pieces must be punched with a leopard's head, showing that the gold was of the "touch of Paris" (a reference to the standard adopted some years previously in France), and silver of "esterling allay". All objects of silver from "all the good towns of England" were to be taken to the City of London to be assayed and to receive the punch of the leopard's head. Thus came into being the first British hall-mark, the leo-pard's head or King's mark. All silver made in England between 1300 and 1363 should, therefore, bear this single mark. Later it was joined by others, and between the years 1478 and 1821 was surmounted by a crown.

Although the ancient guild of London goldsmiths had existed as a thriving and a powerful body of craftsmen for many years, it was not until 1327 that Edward III granted a charter to "The Wardens and Commonalty of the Mystery of Goldsmiths of the City of London", the word "mystery" being derived from the Latin ministerium, meaning trade or craft. The granting of the charter stemmed directly from the regulations laid down in the Act of 1300, which had resulted in petitions by the goldsmiths complaining that they now had to melt down inferior imported plate in order to ascertain its true value. Some goldsmiths were also working secretly and producing fraudulent base alloys and plated tin. The charter emphasised the provisions of the Act and further added "that those of the trade may by virtue of these presents elect honest sufficient men, best skilled in the trade, to enquire of the matters aforesaid and that they who are chosen reform what defects they shall find, and inflict punishment on the offenders . . ."

The chief responsibilities were, therefore, those derived from the original six responsible goldsmiths, namely to ensure the soundness of craftsmanship and the purity of the metals. The new Company later built themselves a hall in the City of London, from which originates the term hall-marking. The first preserved entry in its records appeared some seven years later after the granting of the charter and dealt with ordinary trading events. Over the years such records have provided a wealth of informative material on the history and development generally of the goldsmiths' craft. To this day it is one of the most revered and respected Guilds in England.

Although there are more scientific methods known today for the assaying of gold and silver, the earliest method, that of the ancient touchstone, is still in use for the assaying of gold, both in England and other countries. This simple method consists of rubbing the metal on a touchstone (originally a basaltic rock brought from Mount Tonolus in Lydia) and comparing the pieces of fine metal which are rubbed off, with the rubbings of gold of approved purity. Practically any hard black stone, or even earthenware, can be used as a touchstone. The firm of Josiah Wedgwood produced touchstones of artificial basalte ". . . nearly of the same colour as the natural one; it strikes fire with steel; resists the attacks of the strongest acids . . . and is a touchstone to copper, silver and gold". (From the Wedgwood and Bentley 1779 Catalogue of Intaglios.)

The traditional technique for testing silver, known as cupelation, came into being in the 15th century. A scraping is taken from the silver and weighed. It is then wrapped in lead, placed into a porous cup or cupel and heated in a kiln. The surrounding lead and alloy in the silver then becomes absorbed by the cupel, and

44. A Victorian silver tea pot bearing a Birmingham
hall-mark, 1861. Designed by John Hardman
Powell in imitation of Pugin and made by John
Hardman and Company. (Victoria and Albert
Museum)

45. A three-piece Victorian tea service, made by J. Angell, London, 1844. (S. J. Shrubsole Ltd.)

46. A tea and coffee service, c. 1858. (Garrard and Company Ltd.)

47. A Victorian tea caddy, by WH, 1843. (Garrard and Company Ltd.)

48. Typical Victorian spoon designs, illustrating the unabashed use of mixed decoration from past periods.

49. Sheffield plate cake basket, c. 1760. (Victoria and Albert Museum)

50. An electro-plated tray, designed by Alfred Stevens, 1860–70. (Victoria and Albert Museum)

51. A good set of hall-marks on the base of a tea
pot, showing the crowned leopard's head
(London), lion passant, date letter, f, (1741)
and makers mark, EG.

London 1478   London 1952/53

52. The leopard's head or King's mark. A statute of 1300 provided that no ware of gold or silver should be sold until tested by the 'Gardiens of the Craft' and struck with the leopard's head. This was used alone until 1363, and later became the mark of origin for London.

53. In 1478 a third mark was introduced, to identify the warden responsible for testing each piece sent to be assayed and marked. This mark was first called the touch warden's mark and took the form of a letter of the alphabet which was changed every year. Consequently it became known as the date letter.

George III   Victoria

54. In 1544, a fourth mark, the lion passant was instituted while Henry VIII was on the throne. This mark was introduced to indicate the difference between the standard of wrought plate (92.5 per cent of fine silver) and the standard of the silver coin of the realm which had then been much debased.

55. A fifth mark was introduced in 1784 when an excise duty was imposed on silver and gold. The reigning sovereign's head was struck on all wares in respect of which duty had been paid. When the duty was abolished in 1890 this mark became obsolete.

56. Examples of complete marks, top, made in Chester by William Dodge during the year 1864, duty on the piece paid; below, Britannia silver made in London by Nethaniel Lock in 1705.

the pure silver remains. This is weighed and compared with the weight of the original sample, thus revealing the amount of base metal.

In 1363 came a further Statute of great importance. Although it repeated various earlier legislations, it also introduced another mark to be placed on all silver, that of the maker's mark. Every master goldsmith, it declared "should have a mark by himself, which mark shall be known by them assigned by the King to survey their work and allay. . . ." Thus all silver objects made between 1364 and 1478 should have two marks, the leopard's head and the maker's mark. Unfortunately, names registered at the London Goldsmiths' Hall before the end of the 17th century cannot now be identified from marks because the plates were destroyed during the Great Fire of 1666.

The third compulsory mark, that of the annual date letter, was introduced in 1478, beginning with a letter A, each letter being added for a year, and then changed for the following letter in the alphabet. The date letter shows the date of marking, not necessarily the date of origin, although this is generally so. Sometimes, however, objects have never been marked (or have been altered since they were marked) and are sent to an assay office and marked at this stage, so that they can be sold legally authenticated. Repetition of letters is avoided by using a different type face, and varying the shape of the shield surrounding the letter. The London assay office changes its date letter in May, and omits J and the last five letters of the alphabet. As other assay offices opened, each office used its own list of date letters and type faces. The type faces used by the London office include the following: 1716–1735, Roman capitals; 1736–1755, Roman lower case; 1756–1775, black letter capitals; 1776–1795, Roman lower case; 1796–1815, Roman capitals; 1816–1835, Roman lower case; 1836–1855, black letter capitals.

During the following century, around 1544, a further mark became legalised. This was the lion passant, which was punched on the object to indicate that the metal was of sterling quality. It walks towards the left, then showing a full frontal of the face.

As more silverware was produced it became impracticable for the goods to be taken from various parts of the country to London for the necessary punches. At Chester, a Guild of Goldsmiths

H

supervised the standard of plate as early as the beginning of the 15th century, although this was not regularised until towards the close of the 17th century. At the ancient city of Exeter, silver plate had been produced from the earliest times, and the Exeter assay marks date from the middle of the 16th century, although this office closed towards the end of the 19th century, its last marks generally appearing on pieces assayed in 1882. Silver was also assayed in the old Yorkshire capital of York as early as the middle of the 16th century, and this office also closed in the 19th century, in 1856. At Newcastle-upon-Tyne, silver was assayed from the middle of the 17th century, this office's final marks being struck generally in 1883. Two comparatively new assay offices, the opening of which were necessitated by methods of mass-production which evolved towards the end of the 18th century, were Birmingham and Sheffield. Both were established by an Act of Parliament in 1773, and are still assaying silver today.

The final addition to the specified hall-marks appeared in 1784. This was the sovereign's head. It showed that duty had been paid on all pieces bearing it. By an Act of 1784, a duty was levied of eight shillings on every ounce of gold plate and sixpence on every ounce of silver. The sovereign's head remained in use until 1890, except on various small objects which were not dutiable because of their size.

On Irish silver the sovereign's head did not appear until much later, 1807, and continuing until 1890. A tax imposed by the Irish Government on certain pieces of silver and gold to raise money for improvements to agriculture was indicated by a mark showing the figure of Hibernia, never to be confused with the English Britannia mark. Following the Union of 1800, the sovereign's head superseded this as a duty mark and Hibernia became the town mark of Dublin. Glasgow silver was not punched with the sovereign's head until even later, in 1819.

Today, the sovereign's head is still occasionally used, but not to show that duty has been paid. These are now commemorative marks, like the heads of King George V and Queen Mary which may be found on silver plate for the years 1933–4–5, which commemorate the 25th anniversary of their Accession. The head of Queen Elizabeth II is also found on silver assayed in 1953 to commemorate her Accession. Because most of the assay offices do not change the date letter until about the middle of the year, silver bearing the letter for 1952 can also be found with this mark. Silver made in 1977 bearing the Queen's head commemorates her Silver Jubilee.

Thus, by 1784 a complete set of London hall-marks included five punches. These should appear on all silver of the period which is especially popular with many collectors, i.e., the late 18th century right through to the late 19th century. They are: the leopard's head, the lion passant, the date letter, the sovereign's head and the maker's mark. Sometimes it happens that these marks are incomplete. Perhaps the maker's mark might be missing, or the date letter or even the place of origin. This need not be of any significance, but it is naturally advisable to have the complete set of hall-marks on a piece in which one is investing a lot of money.

The standard for sterling silver consists of 11 ounces 2 pennyweights of fine silver alloyed with 18 pennyweights of copper to the troy pound of 12 ounces. This is known as 925 fine, and has been with one exception the standard for sterling silver since 1300. That exception was during the years 1697–1720, when the Government raised the standard of silver to 958 fine by an Act which came into force on 25 March 1697. One of the most important reasons for the Act was that the growing demand for domestic silver and the shortage of bullion led silversmiths to clip and melt down coins. The Act differentiated between the quality required for coinage and silver plate, raising it for the latter, and thus preventing the easy conversion from coins to plate.

With the new Act came a change in hall-marks. During these years, known as the Britannia high standard period, the leopard's head and the lion passant were replaced by the figure of Britannia, to show that the silver was of the new high standard, and the figure of a lion's head erased. The maker's mark was also regularised enforcing the use of the first two letters of his surname. The Act did not apply to the provincial and Irish assay offices. Because of this the Britannia Standard (Provincial Offices) Act came into being in 1700, which among other things stated that all plate "except such things as by reason of their smallness are not capable of receiving a touch" manufactured after 29 September 1701, shall be punched with marks similar to those used in London, but with the addition of the arms of the city.

As these Acts did not apply to the Irish assay offices, the Britannia standard was never used there. Neither does it appear on Scottish silver because the Act of Union did not become effective until 1707. In 1719, the Wrought Plate Act, which became effective in 1720, restored the standard to its original 925 fine parts. The high standard was permitted as an alternative. The hallmarks reverted to the leopard's head and the lion passant, and makers' marks generally returned to initials. Until 1821, the lion passant, as previously described (referred to as passant guardant) walked to the left, showing the front of his face. After 1821, the lion passant, although still walking to the left, now faced the same direction.

Some pieces of silver possess no hall-marks. An Act was passed exempting from assay numerous small items. The Act decreed the exemption of such things that "by reasons of the smallness or thinness thereof are not capable of receiving the marks hereinbefore mentioned, or any of them, and not weighing ten pennyweights of gold or silver each". In 1790 the position was further clarified, and filigree work was included in the list as well as anything weighing less than 5 pennyweights of silver, except the necks, collars and tops for casters, cruets, glasses and so on. Filigree caddy spoons were thus left unmarked, while ordinary caddy spoons were not.

Although at one time there were no less than nine principal assay offices throughout England, as well as several minor ones, today three principal offices remain, London, Birmingham and Sheffield. London has always been the most important, and the silver made by London craftsmen of the highest quality. London silversmiths jealously guarded their reputation, and won acclaim throughout the world. Their work has embraced every aspect of the silversmith's craft.

Chester possessed its own Company of Goldsmiths who were responsible for the city's hall-marking. Reference to Chester in connection with silver can be traced back to the Domesday Book, which mentions Chester as having mint masters and silver coins. Coins were certainly struck there until the middle of the 17th century, although assaying was not authorised until towards the end of that century. The marks used were similar to those on London silver, with the addition of the Arms of the City of

Chester, and on early pieces assayed towards the end of the 17th century the word "sterling" appeared impressed in a decorative shield. Small items made at Chester included some very nice cream jugs. After 1700, the arms of the city were changed from a sword erect between three wheat sheaves, contained in a decorative shield, to a plain dimidiated shield bearing three lions of England down one side and a wheat sheaf the other. This mark was replaced in 1779 by the original one, namely the sword erect between three wheat sheaves, which continued to be used. When the sovereign's head duty mark was added in 1784, silver assayed at Chester was punched with six marks: town mark, lion passant, leopard's head, date letter, maker's mark and duty mark. After 1839, the leopard's head was discontinued, which means that any silver with the Chester coat-of-arms and leopard's head upon it was probably made between 1779 and 1839.

The Birmingham assay office, as previously mentioned, was established in 1773, and this was only after extremely vigorous campaigning on the part of leading craftsmen like Matthew Boulton. Silversmiths in the area were growing extremely restless with their lot as regards assaying. Owing to new and speedier manufacturing methods the number of their products was increasing rapidly, yet despite the fact that their wares were reaching unprecedented quantities, they still had to travel all the way to Chester (their nearest assay office) for the necessary punches. Quite apart from the length of time which the journey took, sometimes up to a fortnight, there were other tribulations including robbery *en route*, and the careless repacking of items by assay officials, sometimes resulting in breakages.

These problems, which were equally as relevant to Sheffield silversmiths, came gradually to a head. At a meeting in London at The Crown and Anchor in the Strand, Matthew Boulton is said to have put forward the idea of tossing a coin to determine which assay mark was to be used. Birmingham should take the anchor and Sheffield the crown, depending on which way the coin dropped. As a result of the Parliamentary Committee's enquiry of 1773, the campaigns led by Matthew Boulton and a petition presented to Parliament, an Act for appointing Wardens and Assay Masters for assaying wrought plate in the towns of Sheffield and Birmingham was passed in that same year. The silversmiths in these areas were described as being "under great difficulties and hardships in the exercise of their trades, for want of assayers in convenient places to assay and touch their wrought plate". The Guardians of the Standard of Wrought Plate were thus justified because of the distances of these two extremely fast-growing manufacturing centres from assay offices. Birmingham is more than a hundred miles from London and over sixty miles from Chester and York. Birmingham's anchor could be struck either vertically or horizontally and was, of course, in addition to the lion passant, the date letter, maker's mark and duty mark. During the year 1797–98, pieces generally were not uncommonly marked with a double duty sovereign's head. This shows that the correct amount of duty, which had doubled that year, had been duly paid.

The Sheffield assay office, which used the crown as its place of origin mark, included several discrepancies among its marks. On small objects, from 1780 to 1853, the crown and date letter might be placed together in an oval or oblong punch. The crown was placed either above or at the side of the letter. Even more confusing, during the years 1815–20, the crown is found upside down, appearing at the bottom of the letter for 1815, and thereafter at the top. Also, for several years after 1798, the sovereign's head is not always contained in an oval; instead the punch traces the shape of the head.

Although Newcastle-upon-Tyne assayed its last pieces of silver in 1883–84, it has been associated with silver since the 13th century, when a mint was established there. Little is known of the very early plate. Three early place-of-origin marks are a single castle, a lion in an horizontal oval walking to the right and three castles in a shield, two above the third. These were used in shields of varying shapes until the office closed. The Company of Goldsmiths of Newcastle-upon-Tyne was incorporated in 1702. During the Britannia period, the three-castle shield of Newcastle accompanied Britannia, the lion's head erased, the date letter and maker's mark. After the Act decreeing a return to the standard of 925 fine parts, the leopard's head (crowned) and the lion passant facing right replaced Britannia and the lion's head erased. It faces left again from about 1727. The leopard appears uncrowned after around 1845. Also, the punch of the sovereign's head duty mark sometimes follows the shape of the head. Collectors of all

types of tea equipage should take particular note of the characteristics of Newcastle marks, since much domestic silver was
stamped at this assay office, particularly tea pots.

York has associations with silver as far back as the 15th century.
Its mark of origin for many years possessed dual characteristics,
i.e. the very early mark being half a leopard's head and half a
fleur-de-lis, while the later mark up until about 1700 was half a
rose (crowned) and half a fleur-de-lis. Both marks were contained
in a round punch. After 1700, when this assay office was re-
established following a period of closure, the arms of the city, a
Greek cross bearing five diminutive lions passant, became the
mark of origin. This was used until the office closed in 1857,
becoming first contained in a shield and as the years progressed in
a circle. During the Britannia period, the hall-marks increased in
number from three to five because of the addition of the Britannia
figure and the lion's head erased. It is interesting to note that
very little silver appears to have been found bearing York marks
for the years from about 1713 until around 1778; after this date,
of course, the lion passant and leopard's head (crowned) were the
marks which replaced Britannia and the lion's head erased. The
leopard's head was no longer used after about 1850, but it is worth
noting that from about 1787, until around 1811, this head is
usually the proud possessor of fine whiskers, which disappear to
re-appear again later in the 19th century. Once again, the
sovereign's head is sometimes enclosed in an oval, sometimes in an
outline of the shape of the head. On articles made in 1803 and
1806, the lion passant has been found to walk to the right. York
silver assayed until around the middle of the 18th century was
usually of a domestic nature, including various pieces of tea
equipage.

Exeter had established itself as a centre for fine silverware in
Elizabethan days, and the early mark of origin, the Roman
capital X, is found on this Tudor silver. Among other variations,
this letter is also found crowned with a circular boss each side of it,
or even completely surrounded by these. In 1701, these marks
were replaced by a three-towered castle, the arms of the city, and
with certain variations this mark of origin was used until the
Exeter office closed in 1882. During the Britannia period, the
figure of Britannia and the lion's head erased were used, together

with the mark of origin, the date letter and the maker's mark. After 1721, the lion passant and leopard's head (crowned) were used to denote the standard of metal. The leopard's head was no longer used after about 1778, when only four marks were punched until the introduction of the sovereign's head in 1784. At Exeter there were often delays in the changing of the sovereign's head, when a new monarch ascended the throne. Sometimes this happened with provincial offices. Thus William IV had been on the throne for four years before his head replaced that of George IV. From 1797 to 1856 the Exeter date letters were the same as those used for London, but were one year later and contained in different shields. Although a great deal of extremely fine plate emitted from the Exeter assay office, including ecclesiastical vessels, tankards, loving cups and caudle cups, among the domestic silver were some very fine tea pots and coffee pots.

Other assay offices which are no longer functioning include: Norwich, a castle surmounting a lion passant, a crowned rose and other variations; Hull, the letter H or the arms of the city, three ducal coronets above each other in a shield; Leeds, the golden fleece; Lincoln, a fleur-de-lis, often in a circle or ellipse or small dots; Poole a scallop shell; Shrewsbury, an uncrowned leopard's head; Taunton, the letter T and a tun.

Scotland and Ireland, being such a distance from London, also had their own assay offices. Scotland possessed one assay office, that of Edinburgh, until towards the last quarter of the 17th century when silver was first assayed in Glasgow. Often, however, silver outside Edinburgh was not marked at all, other than bearing the maker's mark, although Scottish law had long decreed that the purity of silver and its marking should be the responsibility of deacons who were taken from the ranks of master silversmiths. The personal mark of the deacon-silversmith appears on such early Scottish silver. However, so much silver was produced which did not come up to the necessary standard of fineness, that at one time sentence of death was imposed on any silversmith selling plate below the correct standards. Although, as already mentioned, the Silver Standard Act of 1697, which became law before the union of England and Scotland, did not affect Scottish or Irish silver, when the sterling standard was re-introduced in 1720, the Act obligated Scottish silversmiths to conform by raising the quality of their metal from eleven ounces fine to eleven ounces two penny-weights fine in every twelve ounces of silver. The use of the Britannia standard became optional in Scotland as it then was elsewhere.

The Edinburgh goldsmiths were granted assaying powers in 1585. The castle of Edinburgh City was the chosen place-of-origin mark, accompanied by the deacon's mark and the maker's initials. Sometimes, of course, these latter marks are both the same. The castle altered its shape over the years. After about 1617, its central tower was elongated to stand well above the one on either side of it. The first sequence of date letters was adopted in 1681, the number of letters being twenty-five as against the twenty-letter system employed in London. Six years later a royal charter was granted to the city and the Edinburgh Goldsmiths' Incorporation came into being. With it the assay master's initials replaced the deacon's mark, which in its turn was replaced by a thistle in 1759. The sovereign's head duty mark was first struck, as in London, in 1784, although the new monarch's head did not always later appear as promptly as it might. Queen Victoria's head did not appear until she had been on the throne for about four years. A wide miscellanea of silver has been manufactured in this city down the years, including some fine domestic pieces.

The Glasgow mark of origin, the fish, tree and bell, was first struck towards the end of the 17th century, around 1681. The mark is a strange one and is composed of a tree with a bird on its uppermost bow, a hand-bell hanging from its branches and a salmon with a ring in its mouth at the base. It was derived from the burgh arms. Date letters were used from the earliest years, although they were not regular. A correct sequence of date letters began in 1819, at which point the assay office came into being and introduced a full twenty-six letter cycle. The lion rampant of Scotland and the sovereign's head were also added at this time.

There were approximately fifteen other towns in Scotland with their own guilds of hammermen, the silversmiths placing the town mark and their own initials on their pieces. Some objects bear the punches of an assay office as well as these local marks. The towns include: Canongate (now a part of Edinburgh), a stag's head erased; Aberdeen, combinations of the letters A B D and N, sometimes with three castles; Arbroath, a portcullis; Banff, either a shortening of the name or a fish; Dundee, a two-handled vase containing three lilies, also sometimes with the name; Elgin, the name or a shortening of it; Greenock, an anchor, sometimes with a ship or an oak or a shortening of the name; Inverness, the letters INS, and sometimes for about one hundred years between 1715–1815 a cornucopia as well, from about 1740 a dromedary, and after the turn of the 19th century the possible addition of a thistle; Montrose, a five-petalled rose; Perth, a lamb with a flag and later a double-headed eagle; Tain, the name; Wick, the name.

Much fine silver has come from Ireland over the years. Dublin became the home of Huguenot silversmiths after the revocation of the Edict of Nantes in 1685, and their influence is apparent in silver produced during the 18th century. Although an Act decreed in 1605 that all silver made in Ireland was to be assayed and stamped with the lion, harp, castle and maker's emblem, it was not until 1637 that goldsmiths were granted a charter. Three cycles of letters are found from 1638 into the 18th century, but as very little silver of this period survives, most collectors will find articles of tea equipage dating from the later years of the 18th century. The lion passant is not found on Irish silver, and as the relevant Act decreeing the raising of the fineness to the Britannia standard did not apply to Ireland, there is neither the Britannia mark nor the lion's head erased.

Silver bearing Dublin marks was not always made there. The law enforced Irish silversmiths to register their marks with the Goldsmiths' Company of Dublin, so many came from other districts. On the other hand, craftsmen working in outlying areas sometimes simply ignored the regulation. Because of this, Irish silver is often found with no assay marks. Cork silversmiths had their own organisation which, although called the Company of the Society of Goldsmiths of the City of Cork, actually included various other trades. Until 1715, the mark of origin was a ship between two castles, either punched together or separately. After this date, the words sterling, starling or even stirling were used. Occasionally the word "Dollar" appeared.

Although the hall-marking system may appear confusing at first, its basic structure can be learned quite easily. Other details, like those outlined in this chapter, can be assimilated as the collector's knowledge of silver expands. Collecting silver for the tea table can be approached in depth or at a more superficial level, depending on the objective of the collector. But in either case, a knowledge of hall-marks, married with that of the various styles, is vital for success.

Never trust only the hall-marks. These can be faked in a variety of ways. What usually happens is that a set of marks is removed from lesser or broken objects, and carefully incorporated in a fraudulent piece. When buying objects composed of more than one part, for instance, like a tea pot, make sure that all separate pieces agree with each other's marks. They will not all have a complete set of marks, only the largest piece, the remainder should bear a lion passant. Study the pieces carefully to detect any discrepancy, watching out for decoration and that the same style is carried through. Many vessels are quite cunningly converted. A tankard, for instance, can be very easily altered into a hot water jug, complete with lid. Pause a while to examine the marks on the base of the vessel, and to compare them with those on the lid; two different periods might quickly reveal themselves.

Such pitfalls as these should serve to make collectors wary of buying without sufficient knowledge of both style and hall-marks. Yet, enigmatically, it is these very pitfalls which add zest to the chase. Detecting that something is wrong, and knowing the reason why, always results in a great feeling of satisfaction.

Knowing where to look for hall-marks is useful and saves time. Very early silver spoons were marked inside the bowl, close to the stem. When the Act decreed that the maker should add his mark, this was punched on the stem at the back, where also appeared the date letter. When the lion passant was added, he, too, was placed on the stem, usually between the date letter and the mark of the maker. Gradually the marks began to spread along the back of the stem, but usually the date letter was in the centre. The mark of origin stayed in the bowl until towards the end of the 17th century, when it began to appear on the back of the stem by the maker's mark. Tea spoons were struck with their marks close together at the back of the stem usually near the end; earlier examples may have these near the bowl. It was quite common for mid-18th century tea spoons to have only the mark of the lion passant, although after this date the marks are usually fairly complete.

Caddy spoons, because of their many varied shapes and the diversity of their decoration, are found with their marks inside the bowl, behind the stem and in other places appropriate to the actual design. Mote skimmers, because of their perforated bowls, were marked on the back of their stems, not always very successfully owing to the extremely slender and rounded shape, necessary for its function. Thus, the marks on mote skimmers can be very difficult to distinguish. Sugar tongs are often deprived of their marks, or lack certain ones, quite commonly the date letter. This applies more to earlier examples than those made towards the end of the 18th century.

During the 19th century, London hall-marks were made in various sizes, ranging from 6 mm to 1·5 mm (one quarter to one sixteenth of an inch) in height. Because their punches were placed in a frame which contained them all, the smaller ones always appear in regular alignment, being stamped in the one movement; a good point for collectors who can thus detect copies of earlier styles.

GLOSSARY

ACANTHUS LEAVES Leaves used in stylised decoration, particularly during the neo-classical period, 1770–1800.

ALLOY A base metal combined with a precious metal for hardening, or a combination of base metals fused together.

ANTHEMION A motif based on the honeysuckle or branch of date palm (palmette), used in stylised patterns.

APPLIQUÉ WORK Ornamental work, cut from one sheet of metal and applied to another.

ARABESQUE Scrolls and intertwining foliage and figures in stylised line decoration.

ASTRAGAL Small continuous half-round moulding, commonly used with beading and other types of decoration.

BALUSTER Rotund shape, slender towards top.

BOMBÉ Swelling outline giving a rotund effect, rising out of a low waist; usually quite pronounced.

BOSS Round metal knob or stud.

BRIGHT-CUTTING A special type of engraving in which the tool was applied in a slanting direction to produce a faceted effect.

BRITANNIA METAL An alloy of tin, antimony and copper.

BRITANNIA STANDARD New standard of silver slightly finer (95·8 per cent) than sterling (92·5 per cent), compulsory from 1697 to 1720, and optional after this date. Its distinguishing mark is a figure of Britannia.

BURNISHER Tool with extremely hard working surface used to give a final polish to metal.

CARTOUCHE A frame, usually oval in shape and reflecting the decorative trends of the period, in which is inserted coats-of-arms, inscriptions, etc.

CHASE To decorate metal surface into a pattern with hammer and punches.

CHINOISERIES Ornament with Chinese inspired content, used in a simple form towards the end of the 17th century, and with more fantasy during the rococo period.

CUT-CARD WORK Applying by soldering cut-out patterns taken from a separate sheet of silver.

ELECTRO-PLATE The method using electrolysis to coat a base metal with silver.

EMBOSSING Relief decoration which is punched from the back of the metal.

ENGRAVING To cut lines, or a pattern, with a scorper or graver, into metal.

FESTOONS Garlands of fruit or flowers used greatly during the neo-classical revival.

FINIAL The ornament applied at the apex.

FLUTING Half-round parallel channels, vertical, oblique or curved, usually embossed.

GERMAN SILVERWhite metal alloy.

GADROONING Inverted fluting.

KEY PATTERN Repetitive pattern consisting of straight lines intersecting at right angles, much used during the neo-classical period. Derived from Greek architecture.

KNOP Shaped projection on end of spoon stems, etc.

OENOCHOE The classical urn shape of the Greek vessel used for dipping wine from the bowl and filling the wine cups.

OGEE Concave and convex curves.

OVOLO Half-round or curved convex moulding, used on Tudor silver, derived from classical architecture. It became popular again during the Victorian period.

PATERAE Circular, calssical decoration, very popular during neo-classical period.

PLANISH To smooth the surface of metal by beating it with a broad-faced polished hammer.

PYRIFORM   A pear-shaped form of vessel.

REEDING   Thin lines of moulding.

REPOUSSÉ   Ornamental work hammered from the reverse side of the metal.

SHEFFIELD PLATE   Fusing by heat a sheet of silver on to a thicker piece of copper. When both metals, fused as one, were rolled, they expanded equally, becoming a thin sheet of copper with a layer of silver.

STRAPWORK   Interlaced and arabesque or scroll ornament of architectural origin, generally in repeated patterns.

SWAG   Garlands of ribbons or cloth.

TREFOIL   Three leaves (French *trois feuilles*).

VOLUTE   Scroll, characteristic of Ionic capitals.

PUBLIC COLLECTIONS (ENGLAND)

BATH, Holburne of Menstrie Museum
BIRMINGHAM, City Museum and Art Gallery
CAMBRIDGE, Fitzwilliam Museum
LONDON, Goldsmiths' Hall
LONDON, Victoria and Albert Museum
OXFORD, Ashmolean Museum
SHEFFIELD, City Museum (old Sheffield plate)

COLLECTIONS (AMERICA)

ALBANY, N.Y., Institute of History and Art
BOSTON, MASS., Museum of Fine Arts
CAMBRIDGE, MASS., William Hayes Fogg Art Museum, Harvard University
CLEVELAND, OHIO, Museum of Art
DETROIT, MICH., Institute of Arts
MINNEAPOLIS, MINN., Institute of Arts
NEW HAVEN, CONN., Yale University Art Gallery
NEW YORK, N.Y., Museum of the City of New York
NEW YORK, N.Y., Metropolitan Museum of Art
NEW YORK, N.Y., The New-York Historical Society
PHILADELPHIA, PA., Museum of Art
PROVIDENCE, RHODE ISLAND, Rhode Island School of Design
WASHINGTON, D.C., Smithsonian Institution
WORCESTER, MASS., Worcester Art Museum

SELECT BIBLIOGRAPHY

C. L. Avery, *Early American Silver* (Russell and Russell)

Bradbury Frederick, *History of Old Sheffield Plate* (Macmillan)

Eric Delieb, *Investing in Silver* (Barrie and Rockliff)

J. F. Hayward, *Huguenot Silver in England, 1688–1727* (Faber & Faber)

Bevis Hillier, *Pottery and Porcelain, 1700–1914* (Weidenfeld & Nicolson)

Graham Hood, *American Silver* (Praeger)

Bernard and Therle Hughes, *Three Centuries of English Domestic Silver, 1500–1820* (Lutterworth)

Charles James Jackson, *English Goldsmiths and Their Marks* (Batsford)

Charles C. Oman, *English Domestic Silver* (A. & C. Black)

Robert Rowe, *Adam Silver* (Faber & Faber)

David S. Shure, *Hester Bateman* (W. H. Allen)

Gerald Taylor, *Silver* (Penguin Books)

G. M. Trevelyan, *English Social History* (Longmans)

Stephen H. Twining, *The House of Twining* (Twining)

Patricia Wardle, *Victorian Silver and Silver-Plate* (Barrie & Jenkins)

INDEX

Aberdeen, assay office, 121; place-of-origin mark, 121

Adam, James, 18; drawings for silver produced, 18

Adam, Robert, 18, 30, 34–5; drawings for silver produced, 18; influence of, 30, 34–5

American War of Independence, 13–14; tax on tea as one factor leading to, 13–14

Angell, J., 91; decorations on tea services by, 91

Angular shapes and style, appearance of, 94

Arbroath, assay office, 121; place-of-origin mark, 121

Argentine alloy, supersedes copper, 100–1

Art Nouveau movement, 87, 92, 95–7

Ashbee, Charles Robert, 96; founder of School and Guild of Handicraft, 96; staunch believer in traditional craftsmanship of silversmithing, 96–7

Ashforth, Ellis and Company, 102; punch on Sheffield plate, 102

Ashmolean Museum, Oxford, 17, 25, 37

Assay offices, 113, 116–24; mark, 115

Assaying, 111; earliest methods of a. gold and silver, 112

Ayr, assay office, 122; place-of-origin mark, 122

Banff, assay office, 121–2; place-of-origin mark, 121–2

Barratt, O. W., 105; patent applied for processing coating metals with zinc, 105

Bateman, Ann, 32, 58; as silversmith, 32

Bateman, Hester, 32, 58; most famous woman silversmith, 32

Bateman, Jonathan, 32, 58

Bateman, Peter, 32, 58

Bayley, Simeon, 79–80; American basket made by, 79–80

Beading, 69, 84, 93

Bell, John, 90; association with Summerley's Art Manufactures, 90

Benson, J. W., 91

Benson, W. A. S., 97; produces metalwork on commercial scale, 97

Biggs, Richard, 81; American caster made by, 81

Birmingham: importance of, 18; assay office in, 18, 43, 114, 116, 117–18; production of caddy spoons by silversmiths, 41–2

"Bleeding condition", 99–100

Boelen, Jacob, 13; one of earliest known American tea pots made by, 13

Boulsover, Thomas, 98, 101, 106; discovery in method of processing silver-plated copper 98

Boulton, Matthew, 18–19, 33–4, 43, 80, 99–100, 117; Soho works, Birmingham, major factory in production of Sheffield plate, 18, 34, 99, 101; steam-operated rolling-mills, 80

Boulton, M. P. W., 101

Boulton, Matthew Robinson, firm, 101

Boulton and Fothergill, Messrs., 101; punch on Sheffield plate, 101

Bradbury, Frederick, 103; works, *British and Irish Silver Assay Marks, 1544–1959*, 103q.; *History of Old Silver Plate*, 103q.

Bradbury and Sons, Thomas, 91, 101, 104; producer of plated silver, 101

Bridge, John, 91

Briggs, W., 102; crown on wares made by, 102

Bright-cutting, 19, 33, 35, 41, 42, 56, 60, 65, 66, 71

Britannia high standard period, 17, 115–16, 118–19, 121, 122

Britannia metal, 90, 107

Britannia Standard (Provincial Offices) Act, 1700, 115

Broadhead and Atkins, Messrs., 90, 91; silver and silver-plated goods by, 90

Brugnatelli, 105; process of coating two silver medals with gold by electricity, 105

Burt, Benjamin, 29; famed for rococo work, 29; example of tea pot made by, 29

Butter dishes, appearance of, 85

Caddies, *see* Tea caddies

Caddy spoon, 15, 19, 35, 40–3, 124; great demand for, 41; should bear hall-marks, 41; method of making, 41; variety, decoration and characteristics of, 41; jockey-cap design, 41–2; vine leaf design, 42; eagle, 42; war trophy design, 42; hand-shaped, 42; shell-shaped, 42; other types, 42; cities producing, 43; further examples of, 43; finding hall-marks on, 124

Cadman, George, 100; perfects method associated with Sheffield plate, 100